Paterson

By William Carlos Williams

† *City Lights Books*

Paterson

WILLIAM
CARLOS
WILLIAMS

NEW DIRECTIONS

Grateful acknowledgment is made for the following quotations: from *Really The Blues* by Mezz Mezzrow and Bernard Wolfe. Copyright 1946 by Milton Mezzrow and Bernard Wolfe. Reprinted by permission of Random House, Inc.; and from *Poems 1923-1954* by E. E. Cummings, copyright © 1950 by E. E. Cummings, published by Harcourt, Brace and Co.

Portions of *Paterson V* have appeared previously in *Art News*, *The Nation*, *Poems in Folio* and *Spectrum*, to which grateful acknowledgment is given.

The Sappho translation by William Carlos Williams, copyright © 1957 by Poems in Folio.

For permission to reprint a portion of the Mike Wallace interview in which William Carlos Williams appeared, the author and publisher wish also to express thanks to *The New York Post*.

Acknowledgment is also made to Donald C. Gallup, Curator, Collection of American Literature, Yale University Library, and to Hugh Kenner for assistance with the texts; and to the State Library of New Jersey for the use of Earl Horter's drawing of the Passaic Falls on the cover.

Published in Canada by Penguin Books Canada Limited

Manufactured in the United States
New Directions Books are published for James Laughlin by New Directions Publishing Corporation, 80 Eighth Avenue, New York 10011

SIXTEENTH PAPERBOOK PRINTING

AUTHOR'S NOTE

Paterson is a long poem in four parts—that a man in himself is a city, beginning, seeking, achieving and concluding his life in ways which the various aspects of a city may embody—if imaginatively conceived—any city, all the details of which may be made to voice his most intimate convictions. Part One introduces the elemental character of the place. The Second Part comprises the modern replicas. Three will seek a language to make them vocal, and Four, the river below the falls, will be reminiscent of episodes—all that any one man may achieve in a lifetime.

Dr. Williams originally planned that Paterson *would consist of four "Books," and the above note, his "Argument" for the poem, appeared in the first edition of* Book 1 *in 1946. Books 2, 3 and 4 were published in 1948, 1949 and 1951 respectively. Book 5 was published in 1958; somewhat earlier, Dr. Williams had written about it to the publisher as follows:*

"[since completing *Paterson, Four*] I have come to understand not only that many changes have occurred in me and the world, but I have been forced to recognize that there can be no end to such a story I have envisioned with the terms which I had laid down for myself. I had to take the world of Paterson into a new dimension if I wanted to give it imaginative validity. Yet I wanted to keep it whole, as it is to me. As I mulled the thing over in my mind the composition began to assume a form which you see in the present poem, keeping, I fondly hope, a unity directly continuous with the Paterson of *Pat. 1* to *4*. Let's hope I have succeeded in doing so."

Toward the end of 1960 and in the early months of 1961, Dr. Williams was writing to the publisher of his plans

for a sixth section, but illness prevented him from work-
ing on it. Four pages of notes and drafts for Book 6
were found among the poet's papers after his death and
these have been added as an appendix at the end of this
edition.

We add here, for their interest in giving the genesis of
the poem, the first three pages from Chapter 58 of Wil-
liams's Autobiography:

THE POEM PATERSON

Even though the greatest boon a poet grants the world is
to reveal that secret and sacred presence, they will not
know what he is talking about. Surgery cannot assist him,
nor cures. The surgeon must himself know that his sur-
gery is idle. But the object of this continuous scribbling
comes to him also, I can see by his eyes that he acknowl-
edges it.

That is why I started to write *Paterson:* a man is indeed
a city, and for the poet there are no ideas but in things.
But the critics would have it that I, the poet, am not pro-
found and go on with their profundities, sometimes af-
fecting to write poems in their very zeal as thinkers. It
all depends on what you call profound. For I acknowl-
edge it would, in dealing with man and city, require one
to go to some depth in the form for the purpose.

The thinkers, the scholars, thereupon propound ques-
tions upon the nature of verse, answering themselves or
at least creating tension between thoughts. They think,
and to think, they believe, is to be profound. A curious
idea, if what they think is profitable to their thinking
they are rewarded—as thinkers.

But who, if he chose, could not touch the bottom of
thought? The poet does not, however, permit himself to
go beyond the thought to be discovered in the context of

Poet thinks through things .

that with which he is dealing: no ideas but in things. The poet thinks with his poem, in that lies his thought, and that in itself is the profundity. The thought is *Paterson*, to be discovered there.

Therefore the thinker tries to capture the poem for his purpose, using his "thought" as the net to put his thoughts into. Absurd. They are not profound enough to discover that by this they commit a philosophic solecism. They have jumped the track, slipped out of category; no matter what the thought or the value, the poem will be bad, to make a pigeon roar.

The first idea centering upon the poem, *Paterson*, came alive early: to find an image large enough to embody the whole knowable world about me. The longer I lived in my place, among the details of my life, I realized that these isolated observations and experiences needed pulling together to gain "profundity." I already had the river. Flossie is always astonished when she realizes that we live on a river, that we are a river town. New York City was far out of my perspective; I wanted, if I was to write in a larger way than of the birds and flowers, to write about the people close about me: to know in detail, minutely what I was talking about—to the whites of their eyes, to their very smells.

That is the poet's business. Not to talk in vague categories but to write particularly, as a physician works, upon a patient, upon the thing before him, in the particular to discover the universal. John Dewey had said (I discovered it quite by chance), "The local is the only universal, upon that all art builds." Keyserling had said the same in different words. I had no wish, nor did I have the opportunity to know New York in that way, and I felt no loss in that.

I thought of other places upon the Passaic River, but, in the end, the city, Paterson, with its rich colonial history, upstream, where the water was less heavily polluted, won out. The falls, vocal, seasonally vociferous, associated with many of the ideas upon which our fiscal colonial policy shaped us through Alexander Hamilton, interested me profoundly—and what has resulted therefrom. Even today a fruitful locale for study. I knew of these things. I had heard. I had taken part in some of the incidents that made up the place. I had heard Billy Sunday: I had talked with John Reed: I had in my hospital experiences got to know many of the women: I had tramped Garret Mountain as a youngster, swum in its ponds, appeared in court there, looked at its charred ruins, its flooded streets, read of its past in Nelson's history of Paterson, read of the Dutch who settled it.

I took the city as my "case" to work up, really to work it up. It called for a poetry such as I did not know, it was my duty to discover or make such a context on the "thought." To *make* a poem, fulfilling the requirements of the art, and yet new, in the sense that in the very lay of the syllables Paterson as Paterson would be discovered, perfect, perfect in the special sense of the poem, to have it—if it rose to flutter into life awhile—it would be as itself, locally, and so like every other place in the world. For it is in that, that it be particular to its own idiom, that it lives.

The Falls let out a roar as it crashed upon the rocks at its base. In the imagination this roar is a speech or a voice, a speech in particular; it is the poem itself that is the answer.

In the end the man rises from the sea where the river appears to have lost its identity and accompanied by his faithful bitch, obviously a Chesapeake Bay retriever, turns inland toward Camden where Walt Whitman, much traduced, lived the latter years of his life and died. He always said that his poems, which had broken the dominance of the iambic pentameter in English prosody, had only begun his theme. I agree. It is up to us, in the new dialect, to continue it by a new construction upon the syllables.

Book One

: a local pride; spring, summer, fall and the sea; a confession; a basket; a column; a reply to Greek and Latin with the bare hands; a gathering up; a celebration;

in distinctive terms; by multiplication a reduction to one; daring; a fall; the clouds resolved into a sandy sluice; an enforced pause;

hard put to it; an identification and a plan for action to supplant a plan for action; a taking up of slack; a dispersal and a metamorphosis.

Paterson

Preface

"Rigor of beauty is the quest. But how will you find beauty
when it is locked in the mind past all remonstrance?"

> To make a start,
> out of particulars
> and make them general, rolling
> up the sum, by defective means—
> Sniffing the trees,
> just another dog
> among a lot of dogs. What
> else is there? And to do?
> The rest have run out—
> after the rabbits.
> Only the lame stands—on
> three legs. Scratch front and back.
> Deceive and eat. Dig
> a musty bone

For the beginning is assuredly
the end—since we know nothing, pure
and simple, beyond
our own complexities.

> Yet there is
> no return: rolling up out of chaos,
> a nine months' wonder, the city
> the man, an identity—it can't be
> otherwise—an
> interpenetration, both ways. Rolling

up! obverse, reverse;
the drunk the sober; the illustrious
the gross; one. In ignorance
a certain knowledge and knowledge,
undispersed, its own undoing.

        (The multiple seed,
packed tight with detail, soured,
is lost in the flux and the mind,
distracted, floats off in the same
scum)

Rolling up, rolling up heavy with
numbers.

        It is the ignorant sun
rising in the slot of
hollow suns risen, so that never in this
world will a man live well in his body
save dying—and not know himself
dying; yet that is
the design. Renews himself
thereby, in addition and subtraction,
walking up and down.

        and the craft,
subverted by thought, rolling up, let
him beware lest he turn to no more than
the writing of stale poems . . .
Minds like beds always made up,
        (more stony than a shore)
unwilling or unable.

                    Rolling in, top up,
under, thrust and recoil, a great clatter:
lifted as air, boated, multicolored, a
wash of seas —
from mathematics to particulars—

                    divided as the dew,
floating mists, to be rained down and
regathered into a river that flows
and encircles:

                    shells and animalcules
generally and so to man,

                    to Paterson.

The Delineaments of the Giants

I

Paterson lies in the valley under the Passaic Falls
its spent waters forming the outline of his back. He
lies on his right side, head near the thunder
of the waters filling his dreams! Eternally asleep,
his dreams walk about the city where he persists
incognito. Butterflies settle on his stone ear.
Immortal he neither moves nor rouses and is seldom
seen, though he breathes and the subtleties of his
            machinations
drawing their substance from the noise of the pouring
            river
animate a thousand automatons. Who because they
neither know their sources nor the sills of their
disappointments walk outside their bodies aimlessly
            for the most part,
locked and forgot in their desires—unroused.

            —Say it, no ideas but in things—
            nothing but the blank faces of the houses
            and cylindrical trees
            bent, forked by preconception and accident—
            split, furrowed, creased, mottled, stained—
            secret—into the body of the light!

From above, higher than the spires, higher
even than the office towers, from oozy fields
abandoned to grey beds of dead grass,
black sumac, withered weed-stalks,
mud and thickets cluttered with dead leaves—

the river comes pouring in above the city
and crashes from the edge of the gorge
in a recoil of spray and rainbow mists—

    (What common language to unravel?
    . .   combed into straight lines
    from that rafter of a rock's
    lip.)

A man like a city and a woman like a flower
—who are in love. Two women. Three women.
Innumerable women, each like a flower.

                             But

only one man—like a city.

In regard to the poems I left with you; will you be so kind as to
return them to me at my new address? And without bothering to
comment upon them if you should find that embarrassing—for it
was the human situation and not the literary one that motivated
my phone call and visit.

Besides, I know myself to be more the woman than the poet; and
to concern myself less with the publishers of poetry than with . . .
living . . .

But they set up an investigation . . . and my doors are bolted
forever (I hope forever) against all public welfare workers, profes-
sional do-gooders and the like.

    Jostled as are the waters approaching
    the brink, his thoughts
    interlace, repel and cut under,
    rise rock-thwarted and turn aside
    but forever strain forward—or strike
    an eddy and whirl, marked by a
    leaf or curdy spume, seeming
    to forget   .
    Retake later the advance and
    are replaced by succeeding hordes

[handwritten annotations:]

Stream of conciousness narration

from William James psychology — a horizontal articulation of the self.

he says "stream of consc" was the way the mind worked

James thought of thought as transitions, trans. states, not as static Thoughts to be leaped to from another

7

pushing forward—they coalesce now
glass-smooth with their swiftness,
quiet or seem to quiet as at the close
they leap to the conclusion and
fall, fall in air! as if
floating, relieved of their weight,
split apart, ribbons; dazed, drunk
with the catastrophe of the descent
floating unsupported
to hit the rocks: to a thunder,
as if lightning had struck

All lightness lost, weight regained in
the repulse, a fury of
escape driving them to rebound
upon those coming after—
keeping nevertheless to the stream, they
retake their course, the air full
of the tumult and of spray
connotative of the equal air, coeval,
filling the void

And there, against him, stretches the low mountain.
The Park's her head, carved, above the Falls, by the quiet
river; Colored crystals the secret of those rocks;
farms and ponds, laurel and the temperate wild cactus,
yellow flowered   .   .   facing him, his
arm supporting her, by the *Valley of the Rocks*, asleep.
Pearls at her ankles, her monstrous hair
spangled with apple-blossoms is scattered about into
the back country, waking their dreams—where the deer run
and the wood-duck nests protecting his gallant plumage.

In February 1857, David Hower, a poor shoemaker with a large
family, out of work and money, collected a lot of mussels from
Notch Brook near the City of Paterson. He found in eating them

many hard substances. At first he threw them away but at last submitted some of them to a jeweler who gave him twenty-five to thirty dollars for the lot. Later he found others. One pearl of fine lustre was sold to Tiffany for $900 and later to the Empress Eugenie for $2,000 to be known thenceforth as the "Queen Pearl," the finest of its sort in the world today.

News of this sale created such excitement that search for the pearls was started throughout the country. The Unios (mussels) at Notch Brook and elsewhere were gathered by the millions and destroyed often with little or no result. A large round pearl, weighing 400 grains which would have been the finest pearl of modern times, was ruined by boiling open the shell.

> Twice a month Paterson receives
> communications from the Pope and Jacques
> > Barzun
> (Isocrates). His works
> have been done into French
> and Portuguese. And clerks in the post-
> office ungum rare stamps from
> his packages and steal them for their
> childrens' albums   .

Say it! No ideas but in things. Mr.
Paterson has gone away
to rest and write. Inside the bus one sees
his thoughts sitting and standing. His
thoughts alight and scatter—

Who are these people (how complex
the mathematic) among whom I see myself
in the regularly ordered plateglass of
his thoughts, glimmering before shoes and bicycles?
They walk incommunicado, the
equation is beyond solution, yet
its sense is clear—that they may live
his thought is listed in the Telephone
Directory—

And derivatively, for the Great Falls,
PISS-AGH! the giant lets fly! good *Muncie*, too

They craved the miraculous!

A gentleman of the Revolutionary Army, after describing the Falls, thus describes another natural curiosity then existing in the community: In the afternoon we were invited to visit another curiosity in the neighborhood. This is a monster in human form, he is twenty-seven years of age, his face from the upper part of his forehead to the end of his chin, measures *twenty-seven inches,* and around the upper part of his head is twenty-one inches: his eyes and nose are remarkably large and prominent, chin long and pointed. His features are coarse, irregular and disgusting, his voice rough and sonorous. His body is twenty-seven inches in length, his limbs are small and much deformed, and he has the use of one hand only. He has never been able to sit up, as he cannot support the enormous weight of his head; but he is constantly in a large cradle, with his head supported in pillows. He is visited by great numbers of people, and is peculiarly fond of the company of clergymen, always inquiring for them among his visitors, and taking great pleasure in receiving religious instruction. General Washington made him a visit, and asked "whether he was a Whig or a Tory." He replied that he had never taken an *active* part on either side.

A wonder! A wonder!

From the ten houses Hamilton saw when he looked (at the falls!) and kept his counsel, by the middle of the century—the mills had drawn a heterogeneous population. There were in 1870, native born 20,711, which would of course include children of foreign parents; foreign 12,868 of whom 237 were French, 1,420 German, 3,343 English—(Mr. Lambert who later built the Castle among them), 5,124 Irish, 879 Scotch, 1,360 Hollanders and 170 Swiss—

Around the falling waters the Furies hurl!
Violence gathers, spins in their heads summoning
them:

The twaalft, or striped bass was also abundant, and even sturgeon, of a huge bigness, were frequently caught:— On Sunday, August

31, 1817, one seven feet six inches long, and weighing 126 pounds, was captured a short distance below the Falls basin. He was pelted with stones by boys until he was exhausted, whereupon one of them, John Winters, waded into the water and clambered on the back of the huge fish, while another seized him by the throat and gills, and brought him ashore. The *Bergen Express and Paterson Advertiser* of Wednesday, September 3, 1817, devoted half a column to an account of the incident, under the heading, "The Monster Taken."

They begin!
The perfections are sharpened
The flower spreads its colored petals
wide in the sun
But the tongue of the bee
misses them
They sink back into the loam
crying out
—you may call it a cry
that creeps over them, a shiver
as they wilt and disappear:
Marriage come to have a shuddering
implication

Crying out
or take a lesser satisfaction:
a few go
to the Coast without gain—
The language is missing them
they die also
incommunicado.

The language, the language
fails them
They do not know the words
or have not
the courage to use them   .
—girls from

families that have decayed and
taken to the hills: no words.
They may look at the torrent in
       their minds
and it is foreign to them.   .

They turn their backs
and grow faint—but recover!
       Life is sweet
they say: the language!
       —the language
is divorced from their minds,
the language   . .   the language!

If there was not beauty, there was a strangeness and a bold association of wild and cultured life grew up together in the Ramapos: two phases.

In the hills, where the brown trout slithered among the shallow stones, Ringwood—where the old Ryerson farm had been—among its velvet lawns, was ringed with forest trees, the butternut, and the elm, the white oak, the chestnut and the beech, the birches, the tupelo, the sweet-gum, the wild cherry and the hackleberry with its red tumbling fruit.

While in the forest clustered the ironworkers' cabins, the charcoal burners, the lime kiln workers—hidden from lovely Ringwood —where General Washington, gracing any poem, up from Pompton for rest after the traitors' hangings could be at ease—and the links were made for the great chain across the Hudson at West Point.

Violence broke out in Tennessee, a massacre by the Indians, hangings and exile—standing there on the scaffold waiting, sixty of them. The Tuscaroras, forced to leave their country, were invited by the Six Nations to join them in Upper New York. The bucks went on ahead but some of the women and the stragglers got no further than the valley-cleft near Suffern. They took to the mountains there where they were joined by Hessian deserters from the British Army, a number of albinos among them, escaped negro slaves and a lot of women and their brats released in New York City after the British had been forced to leave. They had them in a pen there— picked up in Liverpool and elsewhere by a man named Jackson under contract with the British Government to provide women for the soldiers in America.

The mixture ran in the woods and took the general name, Jackson's Whites. (There had been some blacks also, mixed in, some West Indian negresses, a ship-load, to replace the whites lost when their ship, one of six coming from England, had foundered in a storm at sea. He had to make it up somehow and that was the quickest and cheapest way.)

New Barbadoes Neck, the region was called.

Cromwell, in the middle of the seventeenth century, shipped some thousands of Irish women and children to the Barbadoes to be sold as slaves. Forced by their owners to mate with the others these unfortunates were succeeded by a few generations of Irish-speaking negroes and mulattoes. And it is commonly asserted to this day the natives of Barbadoes speak with an Irish brogue.

> I remember
> a *Geographic* picture, the 9 women
> of some African chief semi-naked
> astraddle a log, an official log to
> be presumed, heads left:

> Foremost
> froze the young and latest,
> erect, a proud queen, conscious of her power,
> mud-caked, her monumental hair
> slanted above the brows—violently frowning.

> Behind her, packed tight up
> in a descending scale of freshness
> stiffened the others

> and then   .   .
> the last, the first wife,
> present! supporting all the rest growing
> up from her—whose careworn eyes
> serious, menacing—but unabashed; breasts
> sagging from hard use   .   .

13

Whereas the uppointed breasts
of that other, tense, charged with
pressures unrelieved   .
and the rekindling they bespoke
was evident.

                    Not that the lightnings
do not stab at the mystery of a man
from both ends—and the middle, no matter
how much a chief he may be, rather the more
because of it, to destroy him at home

    .   .   Womanlike, a vague smile,
unattached, floating like a pigeon
after a long flight to his cote.

Mrs. Sarah Cumming, consort of the Rev. Hopper Cumming, of
Newark, was a daughter of the late Mr. John Emmons, of Portland,
in the district of Maine. . . . She had been married about two
months, and was blessed with a flattering prospect of no common
share of Temporal felicity and usefulness in the sphere which
Providence had assigned her; but oh, how uncertain is the contin-
uance of every earthly joy.

On Saturday, the 20th of June, 1812, the Rev. Cumming rode
with his wife to Paterson, in order to supply, by presbyterial ap-
pointment, a destitute congregation in that place, on the following
day. . . . On Monday morning, he went with his beloved com-
panion to show her the falls of the Passaic, and the surrounding
beautiful, wild and romantic scenery,—little expecting the solemn
event to ensue.

Having ascended the flight of stairs (the Hundred Steps) Mr. and
Mrs. Cumming walked over the solid ledge to the vicinity of the
cataract, charmed with the wonderful prospect, and making various
remarks upon the stupendous works of nature around them. At
length they took their station on the brow of the solid rock, which
overhangs the basin, six or eight rods from the falling water, where
thousands have stood before, and where there is a fine view of the
sublime curiosities of the place. When they had enjoyed the luxury
of the scene for a considerable length of time, Mr. Cumming said,
"My dear, I believe it is time for us to set our face homeward"; and
at the same moment, turned round in order to lead the way. He

instantly heard the voice of distress, looked back and his wife was gone!

Mr. Cumming's sensations on the distressing occasion may, in some measure, be conceived, but they cannot be described. He was on the borders of distraction, and, scarcely knowing what he did, would have plunged into the abyss, had it not been kindly ordered in providence that a young man should be near, who instantly flew to him, like a guardian angel, and held him from a step which his reason, at the time, could not have prevented. This young man led him from the precipice, and conducted him to the ground below the stairs. Mr. Cumming forced himself out of the hands of his protector, and ran with violence, in order to leap into the fatal flood. His young friend, however, caught him once more. . . . Immediate search was made, and diligently continued throughout the day, for the body of Mrs. Cumming; but to no purpose. On the following morning, her mortal part was found in a depth of 42 feet, and, the same day, was conveyed to Newark.

A false language. A true. A false language pouring—a language (misunderstood) pouring (misinterpreted) without dignity, without minister, crashing upon a stone ear. At least it settled it for her. Patch too, as a matter of fact. He became a national hero in '28, '29 and toured the country diving from cliffs and masts, rocks and bridges—to prove his thesis: Some things can be done as well as others.

THE GRRRREAT HISTORY of that

old time Jersey Patriot

N. F. PATERSON!

(N for Noah; F for Faitoute; P for short)

"Jersey Lightning" to the boys.

So far everything had gone smoothly. The pulley and ropes were securely fastened on each side of the chasm, and everything made in readiness to pull the clumsy bridge into position. It was a wooden structure boarded up on both sides, and a roof. It was about two o'clock in the afternoon and a large crowd had gathered—a large crowd for that time, as the town only numbered about four thousand—to watch the bridge placed in position.

That day was a great day for old Paterson. It being Saturday, the mills were shut down, so to give the people a chance to celebrate. Among those who came in for a good part of the celebration was Sam Patch, then a resident in Paterson, who was a boss over cotton spinners in one of the mills. He was my boss, and many a time he gave me a cuff over the ears.

Well, this day the constables were on the look for Patch, because they thought he would be on a spree and cause trouble. Patch had declared so frequently that he would jump from the rocks that he was placed under arrest at various times. He had previously been locked up in the basement under the bank with a bad case of delirium tremens, but on the day the bridge was pulled across the chasm he was let out. Some thought he was crazy. They were not far wrong.

But the happiest man in the town that day was Timothy B. Crane, who had charge of the bridge. Tim Crane was a hotel keeper and kept a tavern on the Manchester side of the Falls. His place was a great resort for circus men. Such famous circus men of the long ago as Dan Rice and James Cooke, the great bareback rider, visited him.

Tim Crane built the bridge because his rival, Fyfield, who kept the tavern on the other side of the falls, was getting the benefit of the "Jacob's Ladder," as it was sometimes called—the "hundred steps," a long, rustic, winding stairs in the gorge leading to the opposite side of the river—it making his place more easy to get to. . . . Crane was a very robust man over six feet tall. He wore side whiskers. He was well known to the other citizens as a man of much energy and no little ability. In his manner he resembled the large, rugged stature of Sam Patch.

When the word was given to haul the bridge across the chasm, the crowd rent the air with cheers. But they had only pulled it half way over when one of the rolling pins slid from the ropes into the water below.

While all were expecting to see the big, clumsy bridge topple over and land in the chasm, as quick as a flash a form leaped out from the highest point and struck with a splash in the dark water below, swam to the wooden pin and brought it ashore. This was the starting point of Sam Patch's career as a famous jumper. I saw that, said the old man with satisfaction, and I don't believe there is another person in the town today who was an eye-witness of that scene. These were the words that Sam Patch said: "Now, old Tim Crane thinks he has done something great; but I can beat him." As he spoke he jumped.

There's no mistake in Sam Patch!

The water pouring still
from the edge of the rocks, filling
his ears with its sound, hard to interpret.
A wonder!

After this start he toured the West, his only companions a fox and a bear which he picked up in his travels.

He jumped from a rocky ledge at Goat Island into the Niagara River. Then he announced that before returning to the Jerseys he was going to show the West one final marvel. He would leap 125 feet from the falls of the Genesee River on November 13, 1829. Excursions came from great distances in the United States and even from Canada to see the wonder.

A platform was built at the edge of the falls. He went to great trouble to ascertain the depth of the water below. He even successfully performed one practice leap.

On the day the crowds were gathered on all sides. He appeared and made a short speech as he was wont to do. A speech! What could he say that he must leap so desperately to complete it? And plunged toward the stream below. But instead of descending with a plummet-like fall his body wavered in the air— Speech had failed him. He was confused. The word had been drained of its meaning. There's no mistake in Sam Patch. He struck the water on his side and disappeared.

A great silence followed as the crowd stood spellbound.

Not until the following spring was the body found frozen in an ice-cake.

He threw his pet bear once from the cliff overlooking the Niagara rapids and rescued it after, down stream.

II

There is no direction. Whither? I
cannot say. I cannot say
more than how. The how (the howl) only
is at my disposal (proposal) : watching—
colder than stone   .

             a bud forever green,
tight-curled, upon the pavement, perfect
in juice and substance but divorced, divorced
from its fellows, fallen low—

                 Divorce is
the sign of knowledge in our time,
divorce! divorce!

           with the roar of the river
forever in our ears (arrears)
inducing sleep and silence, the roar
of eternal sleep   .   .   challenging
our waking—

—unfledged desire, irresponsible, green,
colder to the hand than stone,
unready—challenging our waking:

Two halfgrown girls hailing hallowed Easter,
(an inversion of all out-of-doors) weaving
about themselves, from under
the heavy air, whorls of thick translucencies
poured down, cleaving them away,
shut from the light: bare-
headed, their clear hair dangling—

Two—
        disparate among the pouring
waters of their hair in which nothing is
molten—

two, bound by an instinct to be the same:
ribbons, cut from a piece,
cerise pink, binding their hair: one—
a willow twig pulled from a low
leafless bush in full bud in her hand,
(or eels or a moon!)
holds it, the gathered spray,
upright in the air, the pouring air,
strokes the soft fur—

                Ain't they beautiful!

    Certainly I am not a robin nor erudite,
    no Erasmus nor bird that returns to the same
    ground year by year. Or if I am   .   .
    the ground has undergone
    a subtle transformation, its identity altered.

Indians!

Why even speak of "I," he dreams, which
interests me almost not at all?

                        The theme
is as it may prove: asleep, unrecognized—
all of a piece, alone
in a wind that does not move the others—
in that way: a way to spend
a Sunday afternoon while the green bush shakes.

.   .   a mass of detail
to interrelate on a new ground, difficultly;
an assonance, a homologue

                        triple piled
pulling the disparate together to clarify
and compress

the river, curling, full—as a bush shakes
and a white crane will fly
and settle later! White, in
the shallows among the blue-flowered
pickerel-weed, in summer, summer! if it should
ever come, in the shallow water!

                    On the embankment a short,
compact cone (juniper)
that trembles frantically
in the indifferent gale: male—stands
rooted there   .

The thought returns: Why have I not
but for imagined beauty where there is none
or none available, long since
put myself deliberately in the way of death?

                    Stale as a whale's breath: breath!
Breath!

        Patch leaped but Mrs. Cumming shrieked
        and fell—unseen (though
        she had been standing there beside her husband half
        an hour or more twenty feet from the edge).

        : a body found next spring
        frozen in an ice-cake; or a body
        fished next day from the muddy swirl—

both silent, uncommunicative

Only of late, late! begun to know, to
know clearly (as through clear ice) whence
I draw my breath or how to employ it
clearly—if not well:

                        Clearly!
speaks the red-breast his behest. Clearly!
clearly!

—and watch, wrapt! one branch
of the tree at the fall's edge, one
mottled branch, withheld,
among the gyrate branches
of the waist-thick sycamore,
sway less, among the rest, separate, slowly
with giraffish awkwardness, slightly
on a long axis, so slightly
as hardly to be noticed, in itself the tempest:

Thus

the first wife, with giraffish awkwardness
among thick lightnings that stab at
the mystery of a man: in sum, a sleep, a
source, a scourge   .

                on a log, her varnished hair
trussed up like a termite's nest (forming
the lines) and, her old thighs
gripping the log reverently, that,
all of a piece, holds up the others—
alert: begin to know the mottled branch
that sings   .

certainly NOT the university,
a green bud fallen upon the pavement its
sweet breath suppressed: Divorce (the
language stutters)

                unfledged:

two sisters from whose open mouths
Easter is born—crying aloud,

                        Divorce!

                                While
the green bush sways: is whence
I draw my breath, swaying, all of a piece,
separate, livens briefly, for the moment
unafraid   .   .

        Which is to say, though it be poorly
        said, there is a first wife
        and a first beauty, complex, ovate—
        the woody sepals standing back under
        the stress to hold it there, innate

        a flower within a flower whose history
        (within the mind) crouching
        among the ferny rocks, laughs at the names
        by which they think to trap it. Escapes!
        Never by running but by lying still—

        A history that has, by its den in the
        rocks, bole and fangs, its own cane-brake
        whence, half hid, canes and stripes
        blending, it grins (beauty defied)
        not for the sake of the encyclopedia.

22

Were we near enough its stinking breath
would fell us. The temple upon
the rock is its brother, whose majesty
lies in jungles—made to spring,
at the rifle-shot of learning: to kill

and grind those bones:

These terrible things they reflect:
the snow falling into the water,
part upon the rock, part in the dry weeds
and part into the water where it
vanishes—its form no longer what it was:

the bird alighting, that pushes
its feet forward to take up the impetus
and falls forward nevertheless
among the twigs. The weak-necked daisy
bending to the wind   .   .   .

                          The sun
winding the yellow bindweed about a
bush; worms and gnats, life under a stone.
The pitiful snake with its mosaic skin
and frantic tongue. The horse, the bull
the whole din of fracturing thought
as it falls tinnily to nothing upon the streets
and the absurd dignity of a locomotive
hauling freight—

           Pithy philosophies of
daily exits and entrances, with books
propping up one end of the shaky table—
The vague accuracies of events dancing two
and two with language which they
forever surpass—and dawns
tangled in darkness—

The giant in whose apertures we
cohabit, unaware of what air supports
us—the vague, the particular
no less vague

his thoughts, the stream
and we, we two, isolated in the stream,
we also: three alike—

we sit and talk
I wish to be with you abed, we two
as if the bed were the bed of a stream
—I have much to say to you

We sit and talk,
quietly, with long lapses of silence
and I am aware of the stream
that has no language, coursing
beneath the quiet heaven of
your eyes

which has no speech; to
go to bed with you, to pass beyond
the moment of meeting, while the
currents float still in mid-air, to
fall—
with you from the brink, before
the crash—

to seize the moment.

We sit and talk, sensing a little
the rushing impact of the giants'
violent torrent rolling over us, a
few moments.

If I should demand it, as
it has been demanded of others

and given too swiftly, and you should
consent. If you would consent

       We sit and talk and the
silence speaks of the giants
who have died in the past and have
returned to those scenes unsatisfied
and who is not unsatisfied, the
silent, Singac the rock-shoulder
emerging from the rocks—and the giants
live again in your silence and
unacknowledged desire—

And the air lying over the water
lifts the ripples, brother
to brother, touching as the mind touches,
counter-current, upstream
brings in the fields, hot and cold
parallel but never mingling, one that whirls
backward at the brink and curls invisibly
upward, fills the hollow, whirling,
an accompaniment—but apart, observant of
the distress, sweeps down or up clearing
the spray—

      brings in the rumors of separate
worlds, the birds as against the fish, the grape
to the green weed that streams out undulant
with the current at low tide beside the
bramble in blossom, the storm by the flood—
song and wings—

      one unlike the other, twin
of the other, conversant with eccentricities
side by side, bearing the water-drops
and snow, vergent, the water soothing the air when
it drives in among the rocks fitfully—

25

While at 10,000 feet, coming in over
the sombre mountains of Haiti, the land-locked
bay back of Port au Prince, blue vitreol
streaked with paler streams, shabby as loose
hair, badly dyed—like chemical waste
mixed in, eating out the shores   .   .

He pointed it down and struck the rough
waters of the bay, hard; but lifted it again and
coming down gradually, hit again hard but
remained down to taxi to the pier where
they were waiting—

   (Thence Carlos had fled in the 70's
leaving the portraits of my grandparents,
the furniture, the silver, even the meal
hot upon the table before the Revolutionists
coming in at the far end of the street.)

I was over to see my mother today. My sister, "Billy," was at the
schoolhouse. I never go when she is there. My mother had a sour
stomach, yesterday. I found her in bed. However, she had helped
"Billy" do up the work. My mother has always tried to do her part,
and she is always trying to do something for her children. A few
days before I left I found her starting to mend my trousers. I took
them away from her and said, "Mother, you can't do that for me,
with your crippled head. You know. I always get Louisa or Mrs.
Tony to do that work for me." "Billy" looked up and said, "It's too
bad about you."

I have already told you I helped with the work, did dishes, three
times daily, swept and mopped floors, porches and cleaned yards,
mowed the lawn, tarred the roofs, did repair work and helped
wash, brought in the groceries and carried out the pots and washed
them each morning, even "Billy's" with dung in it, sometimes, and
did other jobs and then it was not uncommon for "Billy" to say:
"You don't do anything here." Once she even said, "I saw you out
there the other morning sweeping porches, pretending you were
doing something."

Of course, "Billy" has been chopped on by the surgical chopper
and has gone through the menopause and she had a stroke of facial

paralysis, but she has always been eccentric and wanted to boss. My Hartford sister said she used to run over her until she became big enough to throsh her. I have seen her slap her husband square in the face. I would have knocked her so far she would not have got back in a week. She has run at me with a poker, etc., but I always told her not to strike, "Don't make that mistake," I would always caution.

"Billy" is a good worker and thorough going but she wants to lay blame—always on the other fellow. I told my buddie, in Hartford, she was just like our landlady, THE PISTOL. He said he had a sister just like that.

As to my mother, she is obsessed with fire. That's why she doesn't want me to stay there, alone, when she is dead. The children have all said for years, she thinks more of me than any child she has.

                                                               T.

      They fail, they limp with corns. I
      think he means to kill me, I don't know
      what to do. He comes in after midnight,
      I pretend to be asleep. He stands there,
      I feel him looking down at me, I
      am afraid!

           Who? Who? Who? What?
      A summer evening?

      A quart of potatoes, half a dozen oranges,
      a bunch of beets and some soup greens.
      Look, I have a new set of teeth. Why you
      look ten years younger   .

      But never, in despair and anxiety,
      forget to drive wit in, in till it discover
      his thoughts, decorous and simple,
      and never forget that though his thoughts
      are decorous and simple, the despair
      and anxiety: the grace and detail of
      a dynamo—

      So in his high decorum he is wise.

A delirium of solutions, forthwith, forces
him into back streets, to begin again:
up hollow stairs among acrid smells
to obscene rendezvous. And there he finds
a festering sweetness of red lollipops—
and a yelping dog:
Come YEAH, Chichi! Or a great belly
that no longer laughs but mourns
with its expressionless black navel love's
deceit . .

They are the divisions and imbalances
of his whole concept, made weak by pity,
flouting desire; they are—No ideas but
in the facts . .

I positively feel no rancour against you, but will urge you toward
those vapory ends, and implore you to submit to your own myths,
and that any postponement in doing so is a lie for you. Delay makes
us villainous and cheap: All that I can say of myself and of others
is that it matters not so much how a man lies or fornicates or even
loves money, provided that he has not a Pontius Pilate but an
hungered Lazarus in his intestines. Once Plotinus asked, "What is
philosophy?" and he replied, "What is most important." The late
Miguel de Unamuno also cried out, not "More light, more light!"
as Goethe did when he was dying, but "More warmth, more
warmth!" I hate more than anything else the mocking stone bowels
of Pilate; I abhor that more than cozening and falsehoods and the
little asps of malice that are on all carnal tongues. That is why I am
attacking you, as you put it, not because I think you cheat or lie
for pelf, but because you lie and chafe and gull whenever you see
a jot of the torn Galilean in a man's intestines. You hate it; it makes
you writhe; that's why all the Americans so dote upon that canaille
word, extrovert. Of course, nature in you knows better as some
very lovely passages that you have written show.

But to conclude, you and I can do without each other, in the
usual way of the sloughy habits and manners of people. I can con-
tinue with my monologue of life and death until inevitable anni-
hilation. But it's wrong. And as I have said, whatever snares I make
for myself, I won't weep over Poe, or Rilke, or Dickinson, or Gogol,
while I turn away the few waifs and Ishmaels of the spirit in this

country. I have said that the artist is an Ishmael; Call me Ishmael, says Melville in the very first line of Moby Dick; he is the wild ass of a man;—Ishmael means affliction. You see, I am always concerned with the present when I read the plaintive epitaphs in the American graveyard of literature and poetry, and in weighing the head and the heart that ached in the land, that you are not. With you the book is one thing, and the man who wrote it another. The conception of time in literature and in chronicles makes it easy for men to make such hoax cleavages. But I am getting garrulous:—

E. D.

III

How strange you are, you idiot!
So you think because the rose
is red that you shall have the mastery?
The rose is green and will bloom,
overtopping you, green, livid
green when you shall no more speak, or
taste, or even be. My whole life
has hung too long upon a partial victory.

But, creature of the weather, I
don't want to go any faster than
I have to go to win.

                              Music it for yourself.

He picked a hairpin from the floor
and stuck it in his ear, probing
around inside—

The melting snow
dripped from the cornice by his window
90 strokes a minute—

He descried
in the linoleum at his feet a woman's
face, smelled his hands,

strong of a lotion he had used
not long since, lavender,
rolled his thumb

about the tip of his left index finger
and watched it dip each time,
like the head

of a cat licking its paw, heard the
faint filing sound it made: of
earth his ears are full, there is no sound

: And his thoughts soared
to the magnificence of imagined delights
where he would probe

as into the pupil of an eye
as through a hoople of fire, and emerge
sheathed in a robe

streaming with light. What heroic
dawn of desire
is denied to his thoughts?

They are trees
from whose leaves streaming with rain
his mind drinks of desire :

     Who is younger than I?
       The contemptible twig?
    that I was? stale in mind
     whom the dirt

    recently gave up? Weak
     to the wind.
    Gracile? Taking up no place,
    too narrow to be engraved
     with the maps

    of a world it never knew,
     the green and
    dovegrey countries of
     the mind.

A mere stick that has
      twenty leaves
against my convolutions.
      What shall it become,

Snot nose, that I have
      not been?
I enclose it and
      persist, go on.

Let it rot, at my center.
      Whose center?
I stand and surpass
      youth's leanness.

My surface is myself.
      Under which
to witness, youth is
      buried. Roots?

Everybody has roots.

We go on living, we permit ourselves
to continue—but certainly
not for the university, what they publish

severally or as a group: clerks
got out of hand forgetting for the most part
to whom they are beholden.

spitted on fixed concepts like
roasting hogs, sputtering, their drip sizzling
in the fire

Something else, something else the same.

He was more concerned, much more concerned with detaching the label from a discarded mayonnaise jar, the glass jar in which some patient had brought a specimen for examination, than to examine and treat the twenty and more infants taking their turn from the outer office, their mothers tormented and jabbering. He'd stand in the alcove pretending to wash, the jar at the bottom of the sink well out of sight and, as the rod of water came down, work with his fingernail in the splash at the edge of the colored label striving to loose the tightly glued paper. It must have been varnished over, he argued, to have it stick that way. One corner of it he'd got loose in spite of all and would get the rest presently: talking pleasantly the while and with great skill to the anxious parent.

Will you give me a baby? asked the young colored woman
in a small voice standing naked by the bed. Refused
she shrank within herself. She too refused. It makes me
too nervous, she said, and pulled the covers round her.

Instead, this:

In time of general privation
a private herd, 20 quarts of milk
to the main house and 8 of cream,
all the fresh vegetables, sweet corn,
a swimming pool, (empty!) a building
covering an acre kept heated
winter long (to conserve the plumbing)
Grapes in April, orchids
like weeds, uncut, at tropic
heat while the snow flies, left
to droop on the stem, not even
exhibited at the city show. To every
employee from the top down
the same in proportion—as many as
there are: butter daily by
the pound lot, fresh greens—even to
the gate-keeper. A special French maid,
her sole duty to groom
the pet Pomeranians—who sleep.

33

Cornelius Doremus, who was baptized at Acquackonock in 1714, and died near Montville in 1803, was possessed of goods and chattels appraised at $419.58½. He was 89 years old when he died, and doubtless had turned his farm over to his children, so that he retained only what he needed for his personal comfort:

24 shirts at .82½ cents, $19.88: 5 sheets, $7.00: 4 pillow cases, $2.12: 4 pair trousers, $2.00: 1 sheet, $1.37½: a handkerchief, $1.75: 8 caps, .75 cents: 2 pairs shoebuckles and knife, .25 cents: 14 pairs stockings, $5.25: 2 pairs "Mittins" .63 cents: 1 linen jacket, .50 cents: 4 pairs breeches, $2.63: 4 waist coats, $3.50: 5 coats, $4.75: 1 yellow coat, $5.00: 2 hats, .25 cents: 1 pair shoes, .12½ cents: 1 chest, .75 cents: 1 large chair, $1.50: 1 chest, .12½ cents: 1 pair andirons, $1.00: 1 bed and bedding, $18.00: 2 pocketbooks, .37½ cents: 1 small trunk, .19½ cents: Kastor hot, .87½ cents: 3 reeds, $1.66: 1 "Quill wheal," .50 cents.

⚹ Who restricts knowledge? Some say
it is the decay of the middle class
making an impossible moat between the high
and the low where
the life once flourished   .   .   knowledge
of the avenues of information—
So that we do not know (in time)
where the stasis lodges. And if it is not
the knowledgeable idiots, the university,
they at least are the non-purveyors
should be devising means
to leap the gap. Inlets? The outward
masks of the special interests
that perpetuate the stasis and make it
profitable.

   They block the release
that should cleanse and assume
prerogatives as a private recompense.
Others are also at fault because
they do nothing.

By nightfall of the 28th, acres of mud were exposed and the water mostly had been drawn off. The fish did not run into the nets. But a black crowd of people could be seen from the cars, standing about under the willows, watching the men and boys on the drained lake bottom . . . some hundred yards in front of the dam.

The whole bottom was covered with people, and the big eels, weighing from three to four pounds each, would approach the edge and then the boys would strike at them. From this time everybody got all they wanted in a few moments.

On the morning of the 30th, the boys and men were still there. There seemed to be no end to the stock of eels especially. All through the year fine messes of fish have been taken from the lake; but nobody dreamt of the quantity that were living in it. Singularly to say not a snake had been seen. The fish and eels seemed to have monopolized the lake entirely. Boys in bathing had often reported the bottom as full of big snakes that had touched their feet and limbs but they were without doubt the eels.

Those who prepared the nets were not the ones who got the most fish. It was the hoodlums and men who leaped into the mud and water where the nets could not work that rescued from the mud and water the finest load of fish.

A man going to the depot with a peach basket gave the basket to a boy and he filled it in five minutes, deftly snapping the vertebrae back of the heads to make them stay in, and he charged the modest sum of .25 cents for the basket full of eels. The crowd increased. There were millions of fish. Wagons were sent for to carry away the heaps that lined both sides of the roadway. Little boys were dragging behind them all they could carry home, strung on sticks and in bags and baskets. There were heaps of catfish all along the walk, bunches of suckers and pike, and there were three black bass on one stick, a silk weaver had caught them. At a quarter past seven a wagon body was filled with fish and eels . . . four wagon loads had been carried away.

At least fifty men in the lake were hard at work and had sticks with which they struck the big eels and benumbed them as they glided along the top of the mud in shoal water, and so were able to hold them until they could carry them out: the men and boys splashed about in the mud. . . . Night did not put an end to the scene. All night long with lights on shore and lanterns over the mud, the work went on.

Moveless
he envies the men that ran
and could run off
toward the peripheries—
to other centers, direct —
for clarity (if
they found it)
                loveliness and
authority in the world—

a sort of springtime
toward which their minds aspired
but which he saw,
within himself—ice bound

and leaped, "the body, not until
the following spring, frozen in
an ice cake"

Shortly before two o'clock August 16, 1875, Mr. Leonard Sand-
ford, of the firm of Post and Sandford, while at work on the im-
provements for the water company, at the Falls, was looking into
the chasm near the wheel house of the water works. He saw what
looked like a mass of clothing, and on peering intently at times as the
torrent sank and rose, he could distinctly see the legs of a man, the
body being lodged between two logs, in a very extraordinary man-
ner. It was in the "crotch" of these logs that the body was caught.
    The sight of a human body hanging over the precipice was indeed
one which was as novel as it was awful in appearance. The news of
its finding attracted a very large number of visitors all that day.

What more, to carry the thing through?

Half the river red, half steaming purple
from the factory vents, spewed out hot,
swirling, bubbling. The dead bank,
shining mud   .

What can he think else—along
the gravel of the ravished park, torn by
the wild workers' children tearing up the grass,
kicking, screaming? A chemistry, corollary
to academic misuse, which the theorem
with accuracy, accurately misses   .   .

He thinks: their mouths eating and kissing,
spitting and sucking, speaking; a
partitype of five   .

He thinks: two eyes; nothing escapes them,
neither the convolutions of the sexual orchid
hedged by fern and honey-smells, to
the last hair of the consent of the dying.

And silk spins from the hot drums to a music
of pathetic souvenirs, a comb and nail-file
in an imitation leather case—to
remind him, to remind him! and
a photograph-holder with pictures of himself
between the two children, all returned
weeping, weeping—in the back room
of the widow who married again, a vile tongue
but laborious ways, driving a drunken
husband   .   .

        What do I care for the flies, shit with them.
        I'm out of the house all day.

        Into the sewer they threw the dead horse.
        What birth does this foretell? I think
        he'll write a novel bye and bye   .

P.   Your interest is in the bloody loam but what
        I'm after is the finished product.

I.   Leadership passes into empire; empire begets in-
     solence; insolence brings ruin.

Such is the mystery of his one two, one two.
And so among the rest he drives
in his new car out to the suburbs, out
by the rhubarb farm—a simple thought—
where the convent of the Little Sisters of
St. Ann pretends a mystery

                              What
irritation of offensively red brick is this,
red as poor-man's flesh? Anachronistic?
                              The mystery
of streets and back rooms—
wiping the nose on sleeves, come here
to dream   .   .

Tenement windows, sharp edged, in which
no face is seen—though curtainless, into
which no more than birds and insects look or
the moon stares, concerning which they dare
look back, by times.

It is the complement exact of vulgar streets,
a mathematic calm, controlled, the architecture
mete, sinks there, lifts here   .
the same blank and staring eyes.

                              An incredible
clumsiness of address,
senseless rapes—caught on hands and knees
scrubbing a greasy corridor; the blood
boiling as though in a vat, where they soak—

Plaster saints, glass jewels
and those apt paper flowers, bafflingly

complex—have here
their forthright beauty, beside:

Things, things unmentionable,
the sink with the waste farina in it and
lumps of rancid meat, milk-bottle-tops: have
here a tranquility and loveliness
Have here (in his thoughts)
a complement tranquil and chaste.

      He shifts his change:

"The 7th, December, this year, (1737) at night, was a large shock
of an earthquake, accompanied with a remarkable rumbling noise;
people waked in their beds, the doors flew open, bricks fell from
the chimneys; the consternation was serious, but happily no great
damage ensued."

      Thought clambers up,
snail like, upon the wet rocks
hidden from sun and sight—
          hedged in by the pouring torrent—
and has its birth and death there
in that moist chamber, shut from
the world—and unknown to the world,
cloaks itself in mystery—

            And the myth
that holds up the rock,
that holds up the water thrives there—
in that cavern, that profound cleft,
          a flickering green
inspiring terror, watching . .

And standing, shrouded there, in that din,
Earth, the chatterer, father of all
speech . . . .

N.B. "In order apparently to bring the meter still more within the sphere of prose and common speech, Hipponax ended his iambics with a spondee or a trochee instead of an iambus, doing thus the utmost violence to the rhythmical structure. These deformed and mutilated verses were called χωλίαμβοι or ίαμβοι σκάζοντες (lame or limping iambics). They communicated a curious crustiness to the style. The choliambi are in poetry what the dwarf or cripple is in human nature. Here again, by their acceptance of this halting meter, the Greeks displayed their acute aesthetic sense of propriety, recognizing the harmony which subsists between crabbed verses and the distorted subjects with which they dealt—the vices and perversions of humanity—as well as their agreement with the snarling spirit of the satirist. Deformed verse was suited to deformed morality."

—*Studies of the Greek Poets,* John Addington Symonds
Vol. I, p. 284

Choliambs: from Catullus'
The poet of Desire

Book Two

Sunday in the Park

I

Outside
                    outside myself
                              there is a world,
he rumbled, subject to my incursions
—a world
              (to me) at rest,
                         which I approach
concretely—

              The scene's the Park
              upon the rock,
              female to the city

—upon whose body Paterson instructs his thoughts
(concretely)

                    —late spring,
              a Sunday afternoon!

—and goes by the footpath to the cliff (counting:
the proof)

              himself among the others,
—treads there the same stones
on which their feet slip as they climb,
paced by their dogs!

laughing, calling to each other—

                    Wait for me!

. . the ugly legs of the young girls,
pistons too powerful for delicacy! .
the men's arms, red, used to heat and cold,
to toss quartered beeves and .

Yah! Yah! Yah! Yah!

—over-riding
the risks:
pouring down!
For the flower of a day!

Arrived breathless, after a hard climb he,
looks back (beautiful but expensive!) to
the pearl-grey towers! Re-turns
and starts, possessive, through the trees,

— that love,
that is not, is not in those terms
to which I'm still the positive
in spite of all;
the ground dry, — passive-possessive

Walking —

Thickets gather about groups of squat sand-pine,
all but from bare rock . .

—a scattering of man-high cedars (sharp cones),
antlered sumac .

—roots, for the most part, writhing
upon the surface
(so close are we to ruin every
day!)
searching the punk-dry rot

44

The body is tilted slightly forward from the basic standing
position and the weight thrown on the ball of the foot,
while the other thigh is lifted and the leg and opposite
arm are swung forward (fig. 6B). Various muscles, aided

from textbook
technical
descript.

Despite my having said that I'd never write to you again, I do so
now because I find, with the passing of time, that the outcome of
my failure with you has been the complete damming up of all my
creative capacities in a particularly disastrous manner such as I
have never before experienced.

Letters from
Cress.
(Actually
letters from
friend of
W.C.W.

For a great many weeks now (whenever I've tried to write po-
etry) every thought I've had, even every feeling, has been struck
off some surface crust of myself which began gathering when I
first sensed that you were ignoring the real contents of my last
letters to you, and which finally congealed into some impenetrable
substance when you asked me to quit corresponding with you
altogether without even an explanation.

Female
reproach
to the male
poet, he
incorp. into
poem.

That kind of blockage, exiling one's self from one's self—have
you ever experienced it? I dare say you have, at moments; and if
so, you can well understand what a serious psychological injury
it amounts to when turned into a permanent day-to-day condition.

woman opp.
by material
+ indust. soc.
striking back
at male poet
she feels doesn't
und. her --
and her proti.
that long has
been dammed
up.

How do I love you? These!

(He hears! Voices . indeterminate! Sees them
moving, in groups, by twos and fours — filtering
off by way of the many bypaths.)

I asked him, What do you do?

*He smiled patiently, The typical American question.
In Europe they would ask, What are you doing? Or,
What are you doing now?*

*What do I do? I listen, to the water falling. (No
sound of it here but with the wind!) This is my entire
occupation.*

No fairer day ever dawned anywhere than May 2, 1880, when the German Singing Societies of Paterson met on Garret Mountain, as they did many years before on the first Sunday in May.

However the meeting of 1880 proved a fatal day, when William Dalzell, who owned a piece of property near the scene of the festivities, shot John Joseph Van Houten. Dalzell claimed that the visitors had in previous years walked over his garden and was determined that this year he would stop them from crossing any part of his grounds.

Immediately after the shot the quiet group of singers was turned into an infuriated mob who would take Dalzell into their own hands. The mob then proceeded to burn the barn into which Dalzell had retreated from the angry group.

Dalzell fired at the approaching mob from a window in the barn and one of the bullets struck a little girl in the cheek. . . . Some of the Paterson Police rushed Dalzell out of the barn [to] the house of John Ferguson some half furlong away.

The crowd now numbered some ten thousand,

"a great beast!"

for many had come from the city to join the conflict. The case looked serious, for the Police were greatly outnumbered. The crowd then tried to burn the Ferguson house and Dalzell went to the house of John McGuckin. While in this house it was that Sergeant John McBride suggested that it might be well to send for William McNulty, Dean of Saint Joseph's Catholic Church.

In a moment the Dean set on a plan. He proceeded to the scene in a hack. Taking Dalzell by the arm, in full view of the infuriated mob, he led the man to the hack and seating himself by his side, ordered the driver to proceed. The crowd hesitated, bewildered between the bravery of the Dean and   .

Signs everywhere of birds nesting, while
in the air, slow, a crow zigzags
with heavy wings before the wasp-thrusts
of smaller birds circling about him
that dive from above stabbing for his eyes

Walking —

46

he leaves the path, finds hard going
across-field, stubble and matted brambles
seeming a pasture—but no pasture
—old furrows, to say labor sweated or
had sweated here   .

                                        a flame,
spent.

            The file-sharp grass   .

When! from before his feet, half tripping,
picking a way, there starts   .
                    a flight of empurpled wings!
—invisibly created (their
jackets dust-grey) from the dust kindled
to sudden ardor!

                    They fly away, churring! until
their strength spent they plunge
to the coarse cover again and disappear
—but leave, livening the mind, a flashing
of wings and a churring song   .

AND a grasshopper of red basalt, boot-long,
tumbles from the core of his mind,
a rubble-bank disintegrating beneath a
tropic downpour

Chapultepec! grasshopper hill!

—a matt stone solicitously instructed
to bear away some rumor
of the living presence that has preceded
it, out-precedented its breath   .

He thinks of an
Aztec insect:
that the Aztecs
didn't see as a
nuisance, but as
a totem:
ceremony +
ritual.

Opp. of now, where
insects in nature
seen as that
nuisance
to be
destroyed.

These wings do not unfold for flight—
no need!
the weight (to the hand) finding
a counter-weight or counter buoyancy
by the mind's wings   .

He is afraid! What then?

Before his feet, at each step, the flight
is renewed. A burst of wings, a quick
churring sound   :

                    couriers to the ceremonial of love!

—aflame in flight!
                    —aflame only in flight!

                              No flesh but the caress!

He is led forward by their announcing wings.

If that situation with you (your ignoring those particular letters
and then your final note) had belonged to the inevitable lacrimae
rerum (as did, for instance, my experience with Z.) its result could
not have been (as it *has* been) to destroy the validity for me myself
of myself, because in that case nothing to do with my sense of
personal identity would have been maimed—the cause of one's
frustrations in such instances being not *in* one's self nor in the other
person but merely in the sorry scheme of things. But since your
ignoring those letters was not "natural" in that sense (or rather since
to regard it as unnatural I am forced, psychologically, to feel that
what I wrote you about, was sufficiently trivial and unimportant and
absurd to merit your evasion) it could not but follow that that
whole side of life connected with those letters should in consequence
take on for my own self that same kind of unreality and inaccess-
ibility which the inner lives of other people often have for us.

[handwritten margin note:] All the Cress letters: dbt. & imposs. of communic. betw. people.

society blocks it.

—his mind a red stone carved to be
endless flight   .
Love that is a stone endlessly in flight,
so long as stone shall last bearing
the chisel's stroke   .

. .   and is lost and covered
with ash, falls from an undermined bank
and — begins churring!
AND DOES, the stone after the life!

The stone lives, the flesh dies
—we know nothing of death.

—boot long
window-eyes that front the whole head,
                        Red stone! as if
a light still clung in them   .

Love

                        combating sleep
                        _____

                        the sleep
piecemeal

Shortly after midnight, August 20, 1878, special officer Goodridge,
when, in front of the Franklin House, heard a strange squealing
noise down towards Ellison Street. Running to see what was the
matter, he found a cat at bay under the water table at Clark's hard-
ware store on the corner, confronting a strange black animal too
small to be a cat and entirely too large for a rat. The officer ran up
to the spot and the animal got in under the grating of the cellar
window, from which it frequently poked its head with a lightning
rapidity. Mr. Goodridge made several strikes at it with his club but
was unable to hit it. Then officer Keyes came along and as soon as
he saw it, he said it was a mink, which confirmed the theory that
Mr. Goodridge had already formed. Both tried for a while to hit
it with their clubs but were unable to do so, when finally officer

49

Goodridge drew his pistol and fired a shot at the animal. The shot evidently missed its mark, but the noise and powder so frightened the little joker that it jumped out into the street, and made down into Ellison Street at a wonderful gait, closely followed by the two officers. The mink finally disappeared down a cellar window under the grocery store below Spangermacher's lager beer saloon, and that was the last seen of it. The cellar was examined again in the morning, but nothing further could be discovered of the little critter that had caused so much fun.

Without invention nothing is well spaced,
unless the mind change, unless
the stars are new measured, according
to their relative positions, the
line will not change, the necessity
will not matriculate: unless there is
a new mind there cannot be a new
line, the old will go on
repeating itself with recurring
deadliness: without invention
nothing lies under the witch-hazel
bush, the alder does not grow from among
the hummocks margining the all
but spent channel of the old swale,
the small foot-prints
of the mice under the overhanging
tufts of the bunch-grass will not
appear: without invention the line
will never again take on its ancient
divisions when the word, a supple word,
lived in it, crumbled now to chalk.

Under the bush they lie protected
from the offending sun—
11 o'clock
                    They seem to talk

50

[Handwritten marginal notes:]

A chant or intonation enters the poetry.

Imitating powerful Chant against poetry from Pound?

The poet is → The one who can

who can interpret the lovers to each other.

—a park, devoted to pleasure : devoted to   .   grasshoppers!

>   3 colored girls, of age! stroll by
>   —their color flagrant,
>   their voices vagrant
>   their laughter wild, flagellant, dissociated
>   from the fixed scene   .

>   But the white girl, her head
>   upon an arm, a butt between her fingers
>   lies under the bush   .   .

>   Semi-naked, facing her, a sunshade
>   over his eyes,
>   he talks with her

>   —the jalopy half hid
>   behind them in the trees—
>   I bought a new bathing suit, just

>   pants and a brassier   :
>   the breasts and
>   the pudenda covered—beneath

>   the sun in frank vulgarity.
>   Minds beaten thin
>   by waste—among

>   the working classes SOME sort
>   of breakdown
>   has occurred. Semi-roused

>   they lie upon their blanket
>   face to face,
>   mottled by the shadows of the leaves

A landscape of lovers

The poet describes

51

upon them, unannoyed,
at least here unchallenged.
Not undignified: .   .

talking, flagrant beyond all talk
in perfect domesticity—
And having bathed

and having eaten (a few
sandwiches)
their pitiful thoughts do meet

in the flesh—surrounded
by churring loves! Gay wings
to bear them (in sleep)

—their thoughts alight,
away
.   .   among the grass

Walking   —

across the old swale—a dry wave in the ground
tho' marked still by the line of Indian alders

.   .   they (the Indians) would weave
in and out, unseen, among them along the stream

.   come out whooping between the log
house and men working the field, cut them
off! they having left their arms in the block-
house, and—without defense—carry them away
into captivity. One old man   .

⎰ Forget it! for God's sake, Cut
⎱ out that stuff   .

[handwritten in left margin: The poet walking. Describing the lovers in the landscape]

[handwritten: Then]

> he rejoins the path and sees, on a treeless
> knoll—the red path choking it—
> a stone wall, a sort of circular
> redoubt against the sky, barren and
> unoccupied. Mount. Why not?

>   A chipmunk,
> with tail erect, scampers among the stones.

> (Thus the mind grows, up flinty pinnacles)

>   but as he leans, in his stride,
> at sight of a flint arrow-head
>   (it is not)
>   —there
> in the distance, to the north, appear
> to him the chronic hills

>   Well, so they are.

>   He stops short:
>   Who's here?

>   To a stone bench, to which she's leashed,
> within the wall a man in tweeds—a pipe hooked in his jaw—is
> combing out a new-washed Collie bitch. The deliberate comb-
> strokes part the long hair—even her face he combs though her
> legs tremble slightly—until it lies, as he designs, like ripples
> in white sand giving off its clean-dog odor. The floor, stone
> slabs, she stands patiently before his caresses in that bare "sea
> chamber"

>   to the right
> from this vantage, the observation tower
> in the middle distance stands up prominently
> from its pubic grove

[handwritten margin note:] On first reading: comfortable satisfied, but: the dog in on a short leash

[handwritten margin note:] John Prufrock an eliadic scene.

[handwritten margin note:] Broken clashed with the phallic tower.

53

[handwritten note at bottom:] Leashing of collie: a restraint on personal freedom

DEAR B.   Please excuse me for not having told you this when I was over to your house. I had no courage to answer your questions so I'll write it. Your dog *is* going to have puppies although I prayed she would be okey. It wasn't that she was left alone as she never was but I used to let her out at dinner time while I hung up my clothes. At the time, it was on a Thursday, my mother-in-law had some sheets and table cloths out on the end of the line. I figured the dogs wouldn't come as long as I was there and none came thru my yard or near the apartment. He must have come between your hedge and the house. *Every few* seconds I would run to the end of the line or peek under the sheets to see if Musty was alright. She was until I looked a minute too late. I took sticks and stones after the dog but he wouldn't beat it. George gave me plenty of hell and I started praying that I had frightened the other dog so much that nothing had happened. I know you'll be cursing like a son-of-a-gun and probably won't ever speak to me again for not having told you. Don't think I haven't been worrying about Musty. She's occupied my mind every day since that awful event. You won't think so highly of me now and feel like protecting me. Instead I'll bet you could kill . . .

> And still the picnickers come on, now
> early afternoon, and scatter through the
> trees over the fenced-in acres   .

>   Voices!
> multiple and inarticulate   .   voices
> clattering loudly to the sun, to
> the clouds. Voices!
> assaulting the air gaily from all sides.

> —among which the ear strains to catch
> the movement of one voice among the rest
> —a reed-like voice
>   of peculiar accent

> Thus she finds what peace there is, reclines,
> before his approach, stroked
> by their clambering feet—for pleasure

                    It is all for
pleasure   .   their feet   .   aimlessly
            wandering

The "great beast" come to sun himself
                            as he may
.   .   their dreams mingling,
aloof

Let us be reasonable!

                    Sunday in the park,
limited by the escarpment, eastward; to
the west abutting on the old road: recreation
with a view! the binoculars chained
to anchored stanchions along the east wall—
            beyond which, a hawk

                            soars!

—a trumpet sounds fitfully.

Stand at the rampart (use a metronome
if your ear is deficient, one made in Hungary
if you prefer)
and look away north by east where the church
spires still spend their wits against
the sky   to the ball-park
in the hollow with its minute figures running
—beyond the gap where the river
plunges into the narrow gorge, unseen

The falls are heard: rushing chaos

—and the imagination soars, as a voice
beckons, a thundrous voice, endless
—as sleep: the voice
that has ineluctably called them—
                    that unmoving roar!

55

churches and factories
                    (at a price)
together, summoned them from the pit .

—his voice, one among many (unheard)
moving under all.

[handwritten: Like the earthquake in Bk I: _____]   The mountain quivers.
Time! Count! Sever and mark time!

[handwritten: The poet trying to measure out in poetry the]

So during the early afternoon, from place
to place he moves,
his voice mingling with other voices
—the voice in his voice
opening his old throat, blowing out his lips,
kindling his mind (more
than his mind will kindle)

                    —following the hikers.

At last he comes to the idlers' favorite
haunts, the picturesque summit, where
the blue-stone (rust-red where exposed)
has been faulted at various levels
                    (ferns rife among the stones)
into rough terraces and partly closed in
dens of sweet grass, the ground gently sloping.

Loiterers in groups straggle
over the bare rock-table—scratched by their
boot-nails more than the glacier scratched
them—walking indifferent through
each other's privacy   .

                    —in any case,
the center of movement, the core of gaiety.

Here a young man, perhaps sixteen,
is sitting with his back to the rock among
some ferns playing a guitar, dead pan   .

The rest are eating and drinking.

                              The big guy
in the black hat is too full to move   .

                              but Mary
is up!
              Come on! Wassa ma'? You got
broken leg?

                      It is this air!
                          the air of the Midi
and the old cultures intoxicates them:
present!

              —lifts one arm holding the cymbals
of her thoughts, cocks her old head
and dances! raising her skirts:

                      La la la la!

What a bunch of bums! Afraid somebody see
you?   .
              Blah!
                      Excrementi!
                          —she spits.
Look a' me, Grandma! Everybody too damn
lazy.

This is the old, the very old, old upon old,
the undying: even to the minute gestures,
the hand holding the cup, the wine
spilling, the arm stained by it:

Describe
The immigrants into
Rutherford

The lost film Viva Mexico

the peon in the lost
Eisenstein film drinking

from a wine-skin with the abandon
of a horse drinking

so that it slopped down his chin?
down his neck, dribbling

over his shirt-front and down
onto his pants—laughing, toothless?

Heavenly man!

A satyrnalia

—the leg raised, verisimilitude   .
even to the coarse contours of the leg, the
bovine touch! The leer, the cave of it,
the female of it facing the male, the satyr—
    (Priapus!)
with that lonely implication, goatherd
and goat, fertility, the attack, drunk,
cleansed   .

Rejected. Even the film
suppressed : but   .   persistent

The picnickers laugh on the rocks celebrating
the varied Sunday of their loves with
its declining light —

Walking —

58

look down (from a ledge) into this grassy
den
        (somewhat removed from the traffic)
                        above whose brows
a moon! where she lies sweating at his side:

                She stirs, distraught,
against him—wounded (drunk), moves
against him (a lump) desiring,
against him, bored   .

flagrantly bored and sleeping, a
beer bottle still grasped spear-like
in his hand   .

while the small, sleepless boys, who
have climbed the columnar rocks
overhanging the pair (where they lie
overt upon the grass, besieged—

careless in their narrow cell under
the crowd's feet) stare down,
                        from history!
at them, puzzled and in the sexless
light (of childhood) bored equally,
go charging off   .

                There where
the movement throbs openly
and you can hear the Evangelist shouting!

                —moving nearer
        she—lean as a goat—leans
        her lean belly to the man's backside
        toying with the clips of his
        suspenders   .

Classic pose of mars + Venus from renaissance painting trans. into proletarian landscape.

59

—to which he adds his useless voice:
until there moves in his sleep
a music that is whole, unequivocal (in
his sleep, sweating in his sleep—laboring
against sleep, agasp!)

                —and does not waken.

Sees, alive (asleep)
        —the fall's roar entering
his sleep (to be fulfilled)

                    reborn
in his sleep—scattered over the mountain
severally   .

       —by which he woos her, severally.

And the amnesic crowd (the scattered),
called about — strains
to catch the movement of one voice   .

                        hears,
           Pleasure! Pleasure!

                       —feels,
half dismayed, the afternoon of complex
voices its own—
            and is relieved
                (relived)

    A cop is directing traffic
    across the main road up
    a little wooded slope toward
    the conveniences:

                    oaks, choke-cherry,
dogwoods, white and green, iron-wood :
humped roots matted into the shallow soil
—mostly gone: rock out-croppings
polished by the feet of the picnickers:
sweetbarked sassafras   .

leaning from the rancid grease:
                    deformity—

—to be deciphered (a horn, a trumpet!)
an elucidation by multiplicity,
a corrosion, a parasitic curd, a clarion
for belief, to be good dogs   :

NO DOGS ALLOWED AT LARGE IN THIS PARK

[handwritten margin note:] chimes w/ description of poetic foot deformed poetic metre And notion of

[handwritten note below:] what the establishment wants people to be

II

Blocked.

              (Make a song out of that: concretely)
By whom?

    In its midst rose a massive church. . .   And it all came
to me then—that those poor souls had nothing else in the world,
save that church, between them and the eternal stony, ungrate-
ful and unpromising dirt they lived by . . . . .

        Cash is mulct of them that others may live
        secure
        . .   and knowledge restricted.

        An orchestral dullness overlays their world

I see they—the Senate, is trying to block Lilienthal and deliver
"the bomb" over to a few industrialists. I don't think they will
succeed but . .   that is what I mean when I refuse to get ex-
cited over the cry, Communist! they use to blind us. It's terri-
fying to think how easily we can be destroyed, a few votes.
Even though Communism is a threat, are Communists any
worse than the guilty bastards trying in that way to under-
mine us?

        We leap awake and what we see
        fells us   .

        Let terror twist the world!

    Faitoute, sick of his diversions but proud of women,
his requites, standing with his back
to the lions' pit,
                (where the drunken
lovers slept, now, both of them)

                              indifferent,
started again wandering—foot pacing foot outward
into emptiness   .   .

        Up there.
                The cop points.
                        A sign nailed
        to a tree: Women.

position of woman in society: oppressed + blocked

                        You can see figures
        moving beyond the screen of the trees and, close
        at hand, music blurts out suddenly.

Walking —
                                                        a
        cramped arena has been left clear at the base
        of the observation tower near the urinals. This
        is the Lord's line: Several broken benches
        drawn up in a curving row against the shrubbery
        face the flat ground, benches on which
        a few children have been propped by the others
        against their running off   .

        Three middle aged men with iron smiles
        stand behind the benches—backing (watching)
        the kids, the kids and several women—and
        holding,
                a cornet, clarinet and trombone,
        severally, in their hands, at rest.
                                There is also,
        played by a woman, a portable organ   .   .

                        Before them an old man,
        wearing a fringe of long white hair, bareheaded,
        his glabrous skull reflecting the sun's
        light and in shirtsleeves, is beginning to
        speak—

calling to the birds and trees!

> Jumping up and down in his ecstasy he beams
> into the empty blue, eastward, over the parapet
> toward the city   .   .

.   .   .   .

Letter from Cress

There are people—especially among women—who can speak only to one person. And I am one of those women. I do not come easily to confidences (though it cannot but seem otherwise to you). I could not possibly convey to any one of those people who have crossed my path in these few months, those particular phases of my life which I made the subject of my letters to you. I must let myself be entirely misunderstood and misjudged in all my economic and social maladjustments, rather than ever attempt to communicate to anyone else what I wrote to you about. And so my having heaped these confidences upon you (however tiresome you may have found them and however far I may yet need to go in the attainment of *complete* self-honesty which is difficult for anyone) was enough in itself to have caused my failure with you to have so disastrous an effect upon me.

Dr. P. - Williams building a reproach into the poem that no - poet who can't build a place for women into his poetic world.

Look, there lies the city!

> —calling with his back
> to the paltry congregation, calling the winds;
> a voice calling, calling   .

> Behind him the drawn children whom his suit
> of holy proclamation so very badly fits,
> winkless, under duress, must feel
> their buttocks ache on the slats of the sodden
> benches.
> > But as he rests, they sing—when
> prodded—as he wipes his prismed brow.
> > > The light
> fondles it as if inclined to form a halo—

Then he laughs:

> One sees him first. Few listen.
Or, in fact, pay the least
attention, walking about, unless some Polock
with his mouth open tries to make it out,
as if it were some Devil (looks into the faces
of a young couple passing, laughing
together, for some hint) What kind of priest
is this? Alarmed, goes off scowling, looking
back.

> This is a Protestant! protesting—as
though the world were his own   .

>   —another,
twenty feet off, walks his dog absorbedly
along the wall top—thoughtful of the dog—
at the cliff's edge above a fifty foot drop   .

.   .   alternately the harangue, followed
by horn blasts surmounting
what other sounds   .   they quit now
as the entranced figure of a man resumes—

But his decoys bring in no ducks—other than
the children with their dusty little minds
and happiest *non sequiturs.*

>   No figure
from the clouds seems brought hovering near

The detectives found a note on the kitchen table addressed to a
soldier from Fort Bragg, N. C. The contents of the letter showed
that she was in love with the soldier, the detective said.

*Love betrayed:
lack of
communicat.*

This is what the preacher said: Don't think
about me. Call me a stupid old man, that's
right. Yes, call me an old bore who talks until
he is hoarse when nobody wants to listen. That's
the truth. I'm an old fool and I know it.

                        BUT . !
You can't ignore the words of Our Lord Jesus
Christ who died on the Cross for us that we
may have Eternal Life! Amen.

                    Amen! Amen!

shouted the disciples standing behind the
benches. Amen!

       —the spirit of our Lord that gives
the words of even such a plain, ignorant fellow
as I a touch of His Own blessed dignity and
and strength among you   . .

I tell you—lifting up his arms—I bring
the riches of all the ages to you here today.

           It was windless and hot in the sun
           where he was standing bareheaded.

              Great riches shall be yours!
I wasn't born here. I was born in what we call
over here the Old Country. But it's the same
people, the same kind of people there as here
and they're up to the same kind of tricks as over
here—only, there isn't as much money
over there—and that makes the difference.

66

My family were poor people. So I started to work
when I was pretty young.
    —Oh, it took me a long time! but
one day I said to myself, Klaus, that's my name,
Klaus, I said to myself, you're a success.
   You have worked hard but you have been
lucky.
            You're
rich—and now we're going to enjoy ourselves.

Hamilton saw more clearly than anyone else with what urgency
the new government must assume authority over the States if it
was to survive. He never trusted the people, "a great beast," as he
saw them and held Jefferson to be little better if not worse than any.

   So I came to America!

Especially in the matter of finances a critical stage presented
itself. The States were inclined to shrug off the debt incurred during
the recent war—each state preferring to undertake its own private
obligations separately. Hamilton saw that if this were allowed to
ensue the effect would be fatal, to future credit. He came out with
vigor and cunning for "Assumption," assumption by the Federal
Government of the national debt, and the granting to it of powers
of taxation without which it could not raise the funds necessary for
this purpose. A storm followed in which he found himself opposed
by Madison and Jefferson.

  But when I got here I soon found out that I
  was a pretty small frog in a mighty big pool. So
  I went to work all over again. I suppose
  I was born with a gift for that sort of thing.
  I throve and I gloried in it. And I thought then
  that I was happy. And I was — as happy
  as money could make me.

     But did it make me GOOD?

And conventional

private interests are low. Hope of salvation --in
the work of lang., of the poet. yet it's blocked.

He stopped to laugh, healthily, and
his wan assistants followed him,
forcing it out—grinning against
the rocks with wry smiles   .

          NO! he shouted, bending
at the knees and straightening himself up
violently with the force of his emphasis—like
Beethoven getting a crescendo out of an
orchestra—NO!

It did *not* make me good. (His clenched fists
were raised above his brows.) I kept on making
money, more and more of it, but it didn't make
me good.

          America the golden!
          with trick and money
                    damned
          like Altgeld sick
                    and molden
          we love thee bitter
                    land

          Like Altgeld on the
                    corner
          seeing the mourners
                    pass
          we bow our heads
                    before thee
          and take our hats
                    in hand

                    And so
one day I heard a voice . . . a voice—just
as I am talking to you here today.   .   .

          .   .   .   .

.   .   .   .   .   .   And the voice said,
Klaus, what's the matter with you? You're not
happy. I am happy! I shouted back,
I've got everything I want. No, it said.
Klaus, that's a lie. You're not happy.
And I had to admit it was the truth. I wasn't
happy. That bothered me a lot. But I was pig-
headed and when I thought it over I said
to myself, Klaus, you must be getting old
to let things like that worry you.

.   .   .   .   .   .   then one day
our blessed Lord came to me and put His hand
on my shoulder and said, Klaus, you old fool,
you've been working too hard. You look
tired and worried. Let me help you.

I am worried, I replied, but I don't know what to
do about it. I got everything that money can
buy but I'm not happy, that's the truth.

And the Lord said to me, Klaus, get rid of your
money. You'll never be happy until you do that.

As a corollary to the famous struggle for assumption lay the
realization among many leading minds in the young republic that
unless industry were set upon its feet, unless manufactured goods
could be produced income for taxation would be a myth.

The new world had been looked on as a producer of precious
metals, pelts and raw materials to be turned over to the mother
country for manufactured articles which the colonists had no choice
but to buy at advanced prices. They were prevented from making
woolen, cotton or linen cloth for sale. Nor were they allowed to
build furnaces to convert the native iron into steel.

Even during the Revolution Hamilton had been impressed by the
site of the Great Falls of the Passaic. His fertile imagination en-
visioned a great manufacturing center, a great Federal City, to
supply the needs of the country. Here was water-power to turn the
mill wheels and the navigable river to carry manufactured goods to
the market centers: a national manufactury.

69

Give up my money!

                —with monotonous insistence
the falls of his harangue hung featureless
upon the ear, yet with a certain strangeness
as if arrested in space

                That would be a hard thing
for me to do. What would my rich friends say?
They'd say, That old fool Klaus Ehrens must
be getting pretty crazy, getting rid of his
cash. What! give up the thing I'd struggled all
my life to pile up—so I could say I was rich?
No! that I couldn't do. But I was troubled
in mind.

        He paused to wipe his brow while
the singers struck up a lively hymn tune.

                  I couldn't eat, I couldn't
sleep for thinking of my trouble so that
when the Lord came to me the third time I was
ready and I kneeled down before Him
and said, Lord, do what you will with me!

Give away your money, He said, and I
will make you the richest man in the world!
And I bowed my head and said to Him, Yea, Lord.
And His blessed truth descended upon me and filled
me with joy, such joy and such riches as I
had never in my life known to that day and I said
to Him, Master!

             In the Name of the Father
and the Son and the Holy Ghost.

                            Amen.

Amen! Amen! echoed the devout assistants.

Is this the only beauty here?
And is this beauty—
torn to shreds by the
lurking schismatists?

Where is beauty among
these trees?
Is it the dogs the owners
bring here to dry their coats?

These women are not
beautiful and reflect
no beauty but gross . .
Unless it is beauty

to be, anywhere,
so flagrant in desire .
The beauty of holiness,
if this it be,

is the only beauty
visible in this place
other than the view
and a fresh budding tree.

So I started to get rid of my money. It didn't take
me long I can tell you! I threw it away with both
hands. And I began to feel better .   .   .   .

—and leaned on the parapet, thinking

From here, one could see him— that
tied man, that cold blooded
murderer   .   April! in the distance
being hanged. Groups at various
vantages along the cliff   .   having
gathered since before daybreak
to witness it.

One kills
for money but doesn't always get it.

Leans on the parapet thinking, while
the preacher, outnumbered, addresses
the leaves in the patient trees   :

The gentle Christ
child of Pericles
and femina practa

Split between
Athens and
the amphyoxus —lowest poss. form
of animal life.

The gentle Christ—
weed and worth
wistfully forthright

Weeps and is
remembered as of
the open tomb

—threw it away with both hands.   .   until
it was gone

—he made a wide motion with both
hands as of scattering money to the winds—

—but the riches that had been given me are
beyond all counting. You can throw them
carelessly about you on all sides—and still
you will have more. For God Almighty has
boundless resources and never fails. There is no
end to the treasures of our Blessed Lord who
died on the Cross for us that we may be saved.
Amen.

The Federal Reserve System is a private enterprise . . . a private
monopoly . . . (with power) . . . given to it by a spineless Con-
gress . . . to issue and regulate all our money.

They create money from nothing and lend it to private business
(the same money over and over again at a high rate of interest),
and also to the Government whenever it needs money in war and
peace; for which we, the people, representing the Government (in
this instance at any rate) must pay interest to the banks in the form
of high taxes.

Suddenly turns to Fed. Reserve Sys. Hamilton being built up as a symbol of all that's bad: power of money over personal freedom

> The bird, the eagle, made himself
> small—to creep into the hinged egg
> until therein he disappeared, all
> but one leg upon which a claw opened
> and closed wretchedly gripping
> the air, and would not—for all
> the effort of the struggle, remain
> inside   .

Witnessing the Falls Hamilton was impressed by this show of
what in those times was overwhelming power . . . planned a stone
aqueduct following a proposed boulevard, as the crow flies, to
Newark with outlets every mile or two along the river for groups
of factories: The Society for Useful Manufactures: SUM, they
called it.

The newspapers of the day spoke in enthusiastic terms of the fine
prospects of the "National Manufactory" where they fondly be-
lieved would be produced all cotton, cassimeres, wall papers, books,
felt and straw hats, shoes, carriages, pottery, bricks, pots, pans and

73

buttons needed in the United States. But L'Enfant's plans were more magnificent than practical and Peter Colt, Treasurer of the State of Connecticut, was chosen in his place.

.   .   .   .   .   The prominent purpose of the Society was the manufacture of cotton goods.

Washington at his first inaugural
.   .   .   .   .   .   wore
a coat of Crow-black homespun woven
in Paterson   .   .   .   .   .   .

In other words, the Federal Reserve Banks constitute a Legalized National Usury System, whose Customer No. 1 is our Government, the richest country in the world. Every one of us is paying tribute to the money racketeers on every dollar we earn through hard work.

.   .   .   .   In all our great bond issues the interest is always greater than the principle. All of the great public works cost more than twice the actual cost, on that account. Under the present system of doing business we SIMPLY ADD 120 to 150 per cent to the stated cost.

The people must pay anyway; why should they be compelled to pay twice? THE WHOLE NATIONAL DEBT IS MADE UP ON INTEREST CHARGES. If the people ever get to thinking of bonds and bills at the same time, the game is up.

If there is subtlety,
you are subtle. I beg your indulgence:
no prayer should cause you anything
but tears. I had a friend   .   .   .
let it pass. I remember when as a child
I stopped praying and shook with fear
until sleep—your sleep calmed me   —

You also, I am sure, have read
Frazer's Golden Bough. It does you
justice—a prayer such as might be made
by a lover who

Address to compound of deity, woman, muse.

74

appraises every feature of his bride's
comeliness, and terror—
terror to him such as one, a man
married, feels toward his bride—

You are the eternal bride and
father—quid pro quo,
a simple miracle that knows
the branching sea, to which the oak
is coral, the coral oak.
The Himalayas and prairies
of your features amaze and delight—

Why should I move from this place
where I was born? knowing
how futile would be the search
for you in the multiplicity
of your debacle. The world spreads
for me like a flower opening—and
will close for me as might a rose—

*Poet looks into
mirror + sees
himself.*

*The core of flower:
Rutherford NJ*

wither and fall to the ground
and rot and be drawn up
into a flower again. But you
never wither—but blossom
all about me. In that I forget
myself perpetually—in your
composition and decomposition
I find my   .   .
                    despair!

.   .   .   .

Whatever your reasons were for that note of yours and for your
indifferent evasion of my letters just previous to that note—the one
thing that I still wish more than any other is that I could see you.
It's tied up with even more than I've said here. And more impor-
tantly, it is the *one* impulse I have that breaks through that film,

that crust, which has gathered there so fatally between my true self and that which can make only mechanical gestures of living. But even if you should grant it, I wouldn't want to see you unless with some little warmth of friendliness and friendship on your part. . . . Nor should I want to see you at your office under any circumstances. That is not what I mean (because I have no specific matter to see you about now as I had when I first called upon you as a complete stranger, nor as I could have had, just before your last note when I wanted so badly to have you go over some of my most faulty poems with me), I have been feeling (with that feeling increasingly stronger) that I shall never again be able to recapture any sense of my own personal identity (without which I cannot write, of course—but in itself far more important than the writing) until I can recapture some faith in the reality of my own thoughts and ideas and problems which were turned into dry sand by your attitude toward those letters and by that note of yours later. That is why I cannot throw off my desire to see you—not impersonally, but in the most personal ways, since I could never have written you at all in a completely impersonal fashion.

W. trying to talk abt. relat. betw. man + woman that is both professional (gynecologist, doctor) and personal

Downhill movement Descent: into old age, into dark past of mind.

Look for the nul
defeats it all

the N of all
equations   .

that rock, the blank
that holds them up

which pulled away—
the rock's

their fall. Look
for that nul

that's past all
seeing

the death of all
that's past

all being   .

Bleak review of all the poets seen during life.

Failure of lang; of the preacher to pay what he means.

Hamilton has triumphed, in the econ. terms

But Spring shall come and flowers will bloom
and man must chatter of his doom   . .

w/ rhyme, mind of poet turned inward

Passage on memory

The descent beckons
                as the ascent beckoned
                        Memory is a kind
of accomplishment
                a sort of renewal
                                even
an initiation, since the spaces it opens are new
places
              'inhabited by hordes
                        heretofore unrealized,

77

memory theme: b/c is great cultural disruption, the past b⇒ implts, crucial, and only recoverable thru memory

of new kinds—
              since their movements
                           are towards new objectives
(even though formerly they were abandoned)

No defeat is made up entirely of defeat—since
the world it opens is always a place
              formerly
                           unsuspected. A
world lost,
              a world unsuspected
                           beckons to new places
and no whiteness (lost) is so white as the memory
of whiteness   .

Echoes the Pisan cantos: the failure of the poetic project and need to rediscover the past.

With evening, love wakens
              though its shadows
                           which are alive by reason
of the sun shining—
              grow sleepy now and drop away
                           from desire   .

Love without shadows stirs now
              beginning to waken
                           as night
advances.

The descent
              made up of despairs
                           and without accomplishment
realizes a new awakening   :
                           which is a reversal
of despair.

For what we cannot accomplish, what
is denied to love,
        what we have lost in the anticipation—
                    a descent follows,
endless and indestructible   .

Listen!   —

            the pouring water!
                        The dogs and trees
            conspire to invent
            a world—gone!

            Bow, wow! A
            departing car scatters gravel as it
            picks up speed!

            Outworn! *le pauvre petit ministre*
            did his best, they cry,
            but though he sweat for all his worth
            no poet has come   .

            Bow, wow! Bow, wow!

            Variously the dogs barked, the trees
            stuck their fingers to their noses. No
            poet has come, no poet has come.
            —soon no one in the park but
            guilty lovers and stray dogs   .

                        Unleashed!

            Alone, watching the May moon above the
            trees   .

Returning to The Tempest as play att. discovery of the new world [handwritten marginal note]

At nine o'clock the park closes. You
must be out of the lake, dressed, in
your cars and going: they change into
their street clothes in the back seats
and move out among the trees   .

The "great beast" all removed
before the plunging night, the crickets'
black wings and hylas wake   .

Missing was the thing Jim had found in Marx and Veblen and
Adam Smith and Darwin—the dignified sound of a great, calm bell
tolling the morning of a new age   .   .   instead,
the slow complaining of a door loose on its hinges.

                    Faitoute, conscious by moments,
rouses by moments, rejects him finally
and strolls off   .

                    That the poem,
the most perfect rock and temple, the highest
falls, in clouds of gauzy spray, should be
so rivaled   .   that the poet,
in disgrace, should borrow from erudition (to
unslave the mind): railing at the vocabulary
(borrowing from those he hates, to his own
disfranchisement)   .
—discounting his failures   .
seeks to induce his bones to rise into a scene,
his dry bones, above the scene, (they will not)
illuminating it within itself, out of itself
to form the colors, in the terms of some
back street, so that the history may escape
the panders

```
.    .    accomplish the inevitable
poor, the invisible, thrashing, breeding
.    debased city
```

Love is no comforter, rather a nail in the
skull

```
.         reversed in the mirror of its
own squalor, debased by the divorce from learning,
its garbage on the curbs, its legislators
under the garbage, uninstructed, incapable of
self instruction         .
```

```
                a thwarting, an avulsion    :
```

—flowers uprooted, columbine, yellow and red,
strewn upon the path; dogwoods in full flower,
the trees dismembered; its women
shallow, its men steadfastly refusing—at
the best   .

```
        The language    .        words
without style! whose scholars (there are none)
.         or dangling, about whom
the water weaves its strands encasing them
in a sort of thick lacquer, lodged
under its flow         .
```

```
                Caught (in mind)
beside the water he looks down, listens!
But discovers, still, no syllable in the confused
uproar: missing the sense (though he tries)
untaught but listening, shakes with the intensity
of his listening         .
```

More abt failure of lang.

Only the thought of the stream comforts him,
its terrifying plunge, inviting marriage—and
a wreath of fur   .

And She   —

Stones invent nothing, only a man invents.
What answer the waterfall? filling
the basin by the snag-toothed stones?

And He   —

Clearly, it is the new, uninterpreted, that
remoulds the old, pouring down   .

And she   —

It has not been enacted in our day!

Le

pauvre petit ministre, swinging his arms, drowns
under the indifferent fragrance of the bass-wood
trees   .

My feelings about you now are those of anger and indignation; and
they enable me to tell you a lot of things straight from the shoulder,
without my usual tongue tied round-aboutness.
   You might as well take all your own literature and everyone else's
and toss it into one of those big garbage trucks of the Sanitation
Department, so long as the people with the top-cream minds and
the "finer" sensibilities use those minds and sensibilities not to make
themselves more humane human beings than the average person,
but merely as means of ducking responsibility toward a better
understanding of their fellow men, except theoretically—which
doesn't mean a God damned thing.

Cress railing against the literary world

          .   and there go the Evangels! (their organ
loaded into the rear of a light truck) scooting
down-hill   .   the children
are at least getting a kick out of *this!*

His anger mounts. He is chilled to the bone.
As there appears a dwarf, hideously deformed—
he sees squirming roots trampled
under the foliage of his mind by the holiday
crowds as by the feet of the straining
minister. From his eyes sparrows start and
sing. His ears are toadstools, his fingers have
begun to sprout leaves (his voice is drowned
under the falls)   .

Poet, poet! sing your song, quickly! or
not insects but pulpy weeds will blot out
your kind.
                    He all but falls   .   .

And She —

Marry us! Marry us!
                    Or! be dragged down, dragged
under and lost

She was married with empty words:
                                    better to
                                    stumble at
                                    the edge
                                    to fall
                                        fall
                                    and be

                            —divorced

from the insistence of place—
                            from knowledge,
from learning—the terms
foreign, conveying no immediacy, pouring down.

83

                                        —divorced
from time (no invention more), bald as an
egg   .

                    and leaped (or fell) without a
language, tongue-tied
                            the language worn out   .

The dwarf lived there, close to the waterfall—
saved by his protective coloring.

Go home. Write. Compose   .

Ha!

Be reconciled, poet, with your world, it is
the,only truth!

Ha!

—the language is worn out.

And She   —
            You have abandoned me!

            —at the magic sound of the stream
            she threw herself upon the bed—
            a pitiful gesture! lost among the words:
            Invent (if you can) discover or
            nothing is clear—will surmount
            the drumming in your head. There will be
            nothing clear, nothing clear   .

            He fled pursued by the roar.

    Seventy-five of the world's leading scholars, poets and philos-
ophers gathered at Princeton last week

*Hurt + shame of not being among
the honored.*

84

83, 84, 85: the dialogue betw the he + she of it.

                    Faitoute ground his heel
           hard down on the stone:

Sunny today, with the highest temperature near 80 degrees; mod-
erate southerly winds. Partly cloudy and continued warm tomorrow,
with moderate southerly winds.

                Her belly   .   her belly is like
                a cloud   .   a cloud
                                    at evening   .

                His mind would reawaken:

He   Me with my pants, coat and vest still on!

She   And me still in my galoshes!

        —the descent follows the ascent—to wisdom
        as to despair.
        A man is under the crassest necessity
        to break down the pinnacles of his moods
        fearlessly —
        to the bases; base! to the screaming dregs,
        to have known the clean air
        From that base, unabashed, to regain
        the sun kissed summits of love!

                            —obscurely
        in to scribble   .   and a war won!

        —saying over to himself a song written
        previously   .   inclines to believe
        he sees, in the structure, something
                                of interest:

On this most voluptuous night of the year
the term of the moon is yellow with no light
the air's soft, the night bird has
only one note, the cherry tree in bloom

makes a blur on the woods, its perfume
no more than half guessed moves in the mind.
No insect is yet awake, leaves are few.
In the arching trees there is no sleep.

The blood is still and indifferent, the face
does not ache nor sweat soil nor the
mouth thirst. Now love might enjoy its play
and nothing disturb the full octave of its run.

Her belly   .   her belly is like a white cloud   .   a
white cloud at evening   .   before the shuddering night!

My attitude toward woman's wretched position in society and
my ideas about all the changes necessary there, were interesting to
you, weren't they, in so far as they made for *literature?* That my
particular emotional orientation, in wrenching myself free from
patterned standardized feminine feelings, enabled me to do some
passably good work with *poetry*—all that was fine, wasn't it—some-
thing for you to sit up and take notice of! And you saw in one of
my first letters to you (the one you had wanted to make use of,
then, in the Introduction to your Paterson) an indication that my
thoughts were to be taken seriously, because that too could be
turned by you into literature, as something disconnected from life.

But when my actual personal life crept in, stamped all over with
the *very same* attitudes and sensibilities and preoccupations that you
found quite admirable as *literature*—that was an entirely different
matter, wasn't it? No longer admirable, but, on the contrary, de-
plorable, annoying, stupid, or in some other way unpardonable;
because those very ideas and feelings which make one a writer with
some kind of new vision, are often the *very same ones* which, in
living itself, make one clumsy, awkward, absurd, ungrateful, con-
fidential where most people are reticent, and reticent where one

86

should be confidential, and which cause one, all too often, to step on the toes of other people's sensitive egos as a result of one's stumbling earnestness or honesty carried too far. And that they *are* the very same ones—that's important, something to be remembered at all times, especially by writers like yourself who are so sheltered from life in the raw by the glass-walled conditions of their own safe lives.

Only my writing (when I write) is myself: only that is the real me in any essential way. Not because I bring to literature and to life two different inconsistent sets of values, as you do. No, *I* don't do that; and I feel that when anyone does do it, literature is turned into just so much intellectual excrement fit for the same stinking hole as any other kind.

But in writing (as in all forms of creative art) one derives one's unity of being and one's freedom to be one's self, from one's relationship to those particular externals (language, clay, paints, et cetera) over which one has complete control and the shaping of which lies entirely in one's own power; whereas in living, one's shaping of the externals involved there (of one's friendships, the structure of society, et cetera) is no longer entirely within one's own power but requires the cooperation and the understanding and the humanity of others in order to bring out what is best and most real in one's self.

That's why all that fine talk of yours about woman's need to "sail free in her own element" as a *poet*, becomes nothing but empty rhetoric in the light of your behavior towards me. No woman will ever be able to do that, completely, until she is able *first* to "sail free in her own element" in living itself—which means in her relationships with men even before she can do so in her relationships with other women. The members of any underprivileged class distrust and hate the "outsider" who is *one of them*, and women therefore— women in general—will never be content with their lot until the light seeps down to them, not from one of their own, but from the eyes of changed male attitudes toward them—so that in the meantime, the problems and the awareness of a woman like myself are looked upon even more unsympathetically by other women than by men.

And that, my dear doctor, is another reason why I needed of you a very different kind of friendship from the one you offered me.

I still don't know of course the specific thing that caused the cooling of your friendliness toward me. But I do know that if you were going to bother with me *at all*, there were only two things for you to have considered: (1) that I was, as I still am, a woman dying of loneliness—yes, really dying of it almost in the same way that people die slowly of cancer or consumption or any other such disease (and with all my efficiency in the practical world continually undermined by that loneliness); and (2) that I needed desperately, and still do, some ways and means of leading a *writer's* life, either by securing some sort of writer's job (or any other job having to do with my cultural interests) or else through some kind of literary journalism such as the book reviews—because only in work and jobs of that kind, can I turn into assets what are liabilities for me in jobs of a different kind.

Those were the two problems of mine that you continually and almost deliberately placed in the background of your attempts to help me. And yet they were, and remain, much greater than whether or not I get my poetry published. I didn't need the *publication* of my poetry with your name lent to it, in order to go on writing poetry, half as much as I needed your friendship in other ways (the very ways you ignored) in order to write it. I couldn't, for that reason, have brought the kind of responsiveness and appreciation that you expected of me (not with any real honesty) to the kind of help from you which I needed so much less than the kind you withheld.

Your whole relationship with me amounted to pretty much the same thing as your trying to come to the aid of a patient suffering from pneumonia by handing her a box of aspirin or Grove's cold pills and a glass of hot lemonade. I couldn't tell you that outright. And how were you, a man of letters, to have realized it when the imagination, so quick to assert itself most powerfully in the creation of a piece of literature, seems to have no power at all in enabling writers in your circumstances to fully understand the maladjustment and impotencies of a woman in my position?

When you wrote to me up in W. about that possible censor job, it seemed a very simple matter to you, didn't it, for me to make all the necessary inquiries about the job, arrange for the necessary interviews, start work (if I was hired) with all the necessary living conditions for holding down such a job, and thus find my life all straightened out in its practical aspects, at least—as if by magic?

But it's never so simple as that to get on one's feet even in the most ordinary practical ways, for anyone on *my* side of the railway tracks—which isn't your side, nor the side of your great admirer, Miss Fleming, nor even the side of those well cared for people like S. T. and S. S. who've spent most of their lives with some Clara or some Jeanne to look after them even when they themselves have been flat broke.

A completely down and out person with months of stripped, bare hardship behind him needs all kinds of things to even get himself in shape for looking for a respectable, important white-collar job. And then he needs ample funds for eating and sleeping and keeping up appearances (especially the latter) while going around for various interviews involved. And even if and when a job of that kind is obtained, he still needs the eating and the sleeping and the carfares and the keeping up of appearances and what not, waiting for his first pay check and even perhaps for the second pay check since the first one might have to go almost entirely for back rent or something else of that sort.

And all that takes a hell of a lot of money (especially for a woman)—a lot more than ten dollars or twenty five dollars. Or else it takes the kind of very close friends at whose apartment one is quite welcome to stay for a month or two, and whose typewriter one can use in getting off some of the required letters asking for interviews, and whose electric iron one can use in keeping one's clothes pressed, et cetera—the kind of close friends that I don't have and never have had, for reasons which you know.

Naturally, I couldn't turn to *you*, a stranger, for any such practical help on so large a scale; and it was stupid of me to have minimized the extent of help I needed when I asked you for that first money-order that got stolen and later for the second twenty five dollars—stupid because it was misleading. But the different kind of help I asked for, *finally* (and which you placed in the background) would have been an adequate substitute, because I could have carried out *those* plans which I mentioned to you in the late fall (the book reviews, supplemented by almost any kind of part-time job, and later some articles, and maybe a month at Yaddo this summer) *without* what it takes to get on one's feet in other very different ways. And the, eventually, the very fact that my name had appeared here and there in the book review sections of a few publications (I'd prefer not to *use* poetry that way) would have enabled me to obtain certain kinds of jobs (such as an O. W. I. job for instance) without all that red tape which affects only obscure, unknown people.

The anger and the indignation which I feel towards you now has served to pierce through the rough ice of that congealment which my creative faculties began to suffer from as a result of that last note from you. I find myself thinking and feeling in terms of poetry again. But over and against that is the fact that I'm even more lacking in anchorage of any kind than when I first got to know you. My loneliness is a million fathoms deeper, and my physical energies even more seriously sapped by it; and my economic situation is naturally worse, with living costs so terribly high now, and with my contact with your friend Miss X having come off so badly.

However, she may have had another reason for paying no attention to that note of mine—perhaps the reason of having found out that your friendliness toward me had cooled—which would have made a difference to her, I suppose, since she is such a great "admirer" of yours. But I don't know. That I'm in the dark about, too; and when I went up to the "Times" last week, to try, on my own, to get some of their fiction reviews (the "Times" publishes so many of those), nothing came of that either. And it's *writing* that I want to do—not operating a machine or a lathe, because with literature more and more tied up with the social problems and social progress (for me, in my way of thinking) any contribution I might be able to make to the wellfare of humanity (in war-time or peace-time) would have to be as a writer, and not as a factory worker.

When I was very young, ridiculously young (of school-girl age) for a critical role, with my mind not at all developed and all my ideas in a state of first-week embryonic formlessness, I was able to obtain book-reviews from any number of magazines without any difficulty—and *all* of them books by writers of accepted importance (such as Cummings, Babette Deutsch, H. D.) whereas now when my ideas have matured, and when I really have something to say, I can get no work of that kind at all. And why is that? It's because in all those intervening years, I have been forced, as a woman not content with woman's position in the world, to do a lot of pioneer *living* which writers of your sex and with your particular social background do not have thrust upon them, and which the members of my own sex frown upon (for reasons I've already referred to)—so that at the very moment when I wanted to return to writing from living (with my ideas clarified and enriched by living) there I was (and still am)—because of that living —completely in exile socially.

I glossed over and treated very lightly (in my first conversation with you) those literary activities of my early girlhood, because the work in itself was not much better than that which any talented college freshman or precocious prep-school senior contributes to her school paper. But, after all, that work, instead of appearing in a school paper where it belonged, was taken so seriously by editors of the acceptably important literary publications of that time, that I was able to average as much as $15 a week, very easily, from it. And I go into that now and stress it here; because you can better imagine, in the light of that, just how I feel in realizing that on the basis of just a few superficials (such as possessing a lot of appealingly youthful sex-appeal and getting in with the right set) I was able to maintain my personal identity as a writer in my relationship to the world, whereas now I am cut off from doing so because it was necessary for me in my living, to strip myself of those superficials.

W. breaks in + interpolates. (any not Nardy's but WCW's. gives specificity

90

You've never had to live, Dr. P—not in any of the by-ways and dark underground passages where life so often has to be tested. The very circumstances of your birth and social background provided you with an escape from life in the raw; and you confuse that protection from life with an *inability* to live—and are thus able to regard literature as nothing more than a desperate last extremity resulting from that illusionary inability to live. (I've been looking at some of your autobiographical works, as this indicates.)

But living (unsafe living, I mean) isn't something one just sits back and decides about. It happens to one, in a small way, like measles; or in a big way, like a leaking boat or an earthquake. Or else it doesn't happen. And when it does, then one must bring, as I must, one's life to literature; and when it doesn't then one brings to life (as you do) purely literary sympathies and understandings, the insights and humanity of words on paper *only*—and also, alas, the ego of the literary man which most likely played an important part in the change of your attitude toward me. That literary man's ego wanted to help me in such a way, I think, that my own achievements might serve as a flower in his buttonhole, if that kind of help had been enough to make me bloom.

But I have no blossoms to bring to any man in the way of either love *or* friendship. That's one of the reasons why I didn't want that introduction to my poems. And I'm not wanting to be nasty or sarcastic in the last lines of this letter. On the contrary a feeling of profound sadness has replaced now the anger and the indignation with which I started to write all this. I wanted your friendship more than I ever wanted anything else (yes, *more*, and I've wanted other things badly) I wanted it desperately, not because I have a single thing with which to adorn any man's pride—but just because I haven't.

Yes, the anger which I imagined myself to feel on all the previous pages, was false. I am too unhappy and too lonely to be angry; and if some of the things to which I have called your attention here should cause any change of heart in you regarding me, that would be just about the only thing I can conceive of as occurring in my life right now.

La votre
C.

Ironic
Mock Romanticism

P. S. That I'm back here at 21 Pine Street causes me to add that that mystery as to who forged the "Cress" on that money order and also took one of Brown's checks (though his was *not* cashed, and therefore replaced later) never did get cleared up. And the janitor who was here at the time, is dead now. I don't think it was he took any of the money. But still I was rather glad that the post-office didn't follow it through because just in case Bob did have anything to do with it, he would have gotten into serious trouble—which I shouldn't have welcomed, because he was one of those miserably underpaid negroes and an awfully decent human being in lots of ways. But now I wish it *had* been followed through *after* he died (which was over two months ago) because the crooks may have been those low vile upstate farm people whose year-round exploitation of down and out farm help ought to be brought to light in some fashion, and because if they *did* steal the money order and were arrested for it, that in itself would have brought to the attention of the proper authorities all their other illegal activities as well: And yet that kind of justice doesn't interest me greatly. What's at the root of this or that crime or antisocial act, both psychologically and environmentally, always interests me more. But as I make that last statement, I'm reminded of how much I'd like to do a lot of things with *people* in some prose—some stories, maybe a novel. I can't tell you how much I want the living which I need in order to write. And I simply can't achieve them entirely alone. I don't even possess a typewriter now, nor have even a rented one —and I can't think properly except on a typewriter. I can do poetry (though only the first draft) in long-hand, and letters. But for any prose writing, other than letters, I can't do any work without a typewriter. But that of course is the least of my problems—the typewriter; at least the easiest to do something about.

C.

Dr. P.:

This is the simplest, most outright letter I've ever written to you; and you ought to read it all the way through, and carefully, be-cause it's about you, as a writer, and about the ideas regarding women that you expressed in your article on A. N., and because in regard to myself, it contains certain information which I did not think it necessary to give you before, and which I do think now you ought to have. And if my anger in the beginning makes you too angry to go on from there—well, that anger of mine isn't there in the last part, now as I attach this post-script.

C.

And if you don't feel like reading it even for those reasons, will you then do so, *please*, merely out of fairness to me—much time and much thought and much unhappiness having gone into those pages.

Book Three

Anais Nin

Cities, for Oliver, were not a part of nature. He could hardly feel, he could hardly admit even when it was pointed out to him, that cities are a second body for the human mind, a second organism, more rational, permanent and decorative than the animal organism of flesh and bone: a work of natural yet moral art, where the soul sets up her trophies of action and instruments of pleasure.

—*The Last Puritan*. SANTAYANA.

The Library

I love the locust tree
the sweet white locust
　　How much?
　　How much?
How much does it cost
to love the locust tree
　　in bloom?

A fortune bigger than
Avery could muster
　　So much
　　So much
the shelving green
　　locust
whose bright small leaves
　　in June
lean among flowers
sweet and white at
　　heavy cost

　　　　　　　A cool of books
will sometimes lead the mind to libraries
of a hot afternoon, if books can be found
cool to the sense to lead the mind away.

For there is a wind or ghost of a wind
in all books echoing the life
there, a high wind that fills the tubes
of the ear until we think we hear a wind,
actual　　.

                              to lead the mind away.

Drawn from the streets we break off
our minds' seclusion and are taken up by
the books' winds, seeking, seeking
down the wind
until we are unaware which is the wind and
which the wind's power over us
                              to lead the mind away

and there grows in the mind
a scent, it may be, of locust blossoms
whose perfume is itself a wind moving
                              to lead the mind away

through which, below the cataract
soon to be dry
the river whirls and eddys
                              first recollected.

Spent from wandering the useless
streets these months, faces folded against
him like clover at nightfall, something
has brought him back to his own
                              mind   .

              in which a falls unseen
tumbles and rights itself
and refalls—and does not cease, falling
and refalling with a roar, a reverberation
not of the falls but of its rumor
                              unabated

                 Beautiful thing,
my dove, unable and all who are windblown,
touched by the fire
                 and unable,

a roar that (soundless) drowns the sense
with its reiteration
                    unwilling to lie in its bed
and sleep and sleep, sleep
                              in its dark bed.

Summer! it is summer   .
—and still the roar in his mind is
unabated

The last wolf was killed near the Weisse Huis in the year 1723

Books will give rest sometimes against
the uproar of water falling
and righting itself to refall filling
the mind with its reverberation
                              shaking stone.

Blow! So be it. Bring down! So be it. Consume
and submerge! So be it. Cyclone, fire
and flood. So be it. Hell, New Jersey, it said
on the letter. Delivered without comment.
So be it!
          Run from it, if you will. So be it.
(Winds that enshroud us in their folds—
or no wind). So be it. Pull at the doors, of a hot
afternoon, doors that the wind holds, wrenches
from our arms — and hands. So be it. The Library
is sanctuary to our fears. So be it. So be it.
— the wind that has tripped us, pressed upon
us, prurient or upon the prurience of our fears
— laughter fading. So be it.
                              Sit breathless
or still breathless. So be it. Then, eased
turn to the task. So be it   :
                              Old newspaper files,

to find — a child burned in a field,
no language. Tried, aflame, to crawl under
a fence to go home. So be it. Two others,
boy and girl, clasped in each others' arms
(clasped also by the water) So be it. Drowned
wordless in the canal. So be it. The Paterson
Cricket Club, 1896. A woman lobbyist. So
be it. Two local millionaires — moved away.
So be it. Another Indian rock shelter
found — a bone awl. So be it. The
old Rogers Locomotive Works. So be it.
Shield us from loneliness. So be it. The mind
reels, starts back amazed from the reading   .
So be it.

       He turns: over his right shoulder
a vague outline, speaking   .

       Gently!   Gently!
       as in all things an opposite
            that awakes
       the fury, conceiving
            knowledge
       by way of despair that has
            no place
       to lay its glossy head—

       Save only—not alone!
            Never, if possible
       alone!   to escape the accepted
            chopping block
       and a square hat !   .

The "Castle" too to be razed. So be it. For no
reason other than that it is *there*, in-
comprehensible;   of no USE! So be it. So be it.

                    Lambert, the poor English boy,
        the immigrant, who built it
                    was the first
                        to oppose the unions:

        This is MY shop. I reserve the right (and he **did**)
        to walk down the row (between his looms) and
        fire any son-of-a-bitch I choose without excuse
        or reason more than that I don't like his face.

Rose and I didn't know each other when we both went to the
Paterson strike around the first war and worked in the Pagent. She
went regularly to feed Jack Reed in jail and I listened to Big Bill
Haywood, Gurley Flynn and the rest of the big hearts and helping
hands in Union Hall. And look at the damned thing now.

        They broke him all right   .

                    —the old boy himself, a Limey,
        his head full of castles, the pivots of that
        curt dialectic (while it lasted), built himself **a**
        Balmoral on the alluvial silt, the rock-fall skirt-
        ing the volcanic upthrust of the "Mountain"

                        —some of the windows
        of the main house illuminated by translucent
        laminae of planed pebbles (his first wife
        admired them) by far the most authentic detail
        of the place; at least the best
        to be had there and the best artifact   .

        The province of the poem is the world.
        When the sun rises, it rises in the poem
        and when it sets darkness comes down
        and the poem is dark   .

*→ like late
Stevensian*

*this not
to say the poet is dead.*

                                    99

and lamps are lit, cats prowl and men
read, read—or mumble and stare
at that which their small lights distinguish
or obscure or their hands search out

in the dark. The poem moves them or
it does not move them.   Faitoute, his ears
ringing . no sound . no great city,
as he seems to read —

                    a roar of books
from the wadded library oppresses him
                                        until
his mind begins to drift   .

                    Beautiful thing:

                    — a dark flame,
a wind, a flood—counter to all staleness.

Dead men's dreams, confined by these walls, risen,
seek an outlet. The spirit languishes,
unable, unable not from lack of innate ability —

                    (barring alone sure death)

but from that which immures them pressed here
together with their fellows, for respite   .

Flown in from before the cold or nightbound
(the light attracted them)
                    they sought safety (in books)
but ended battering against glass
                    at the high windows

The Library is desolation, it has a smell of its own
of stagnation and death   .

Beautiful Thing!

—the cost of dreams.
                in which we search, after a surgery
of the wits and must translate, quickly
step by step or be destroyed—under a spell
to remain a castrate (a slowly descending veil
closing about the mind
                        cutting the mind away   .

                SILENCE !

        Awake, he dozes in a fever heat,
cheeks burning   .   .   loaning blood
to the past, amazed   .   risking life.

And as his mind fades, joining the others, he
seeks to bring it back—but it
eludes him, flutters again and flies off and
again away   .

                O Thalassa, Thalassa!
                the lash and hiss of water

                        The sea!

        How near it was to them!

                Soon!

                        Too soon   .

—and still he brings it back, battering
with the rest against the vents and high windows

(They do not yield but shriek
                              as furies,
shriek and execrate the imagination, the impotent,
a woman against a woman, seeking to destroy
it but cannot, the life will not out of it)   .

A library — of books! decrying all books
that enfeeble the mind's intent

                              Beautiful thing!

The Indians were accused of killing two or three pigs—this was
untrue, as afterward proved, because the pigs had been butchered
by the white men themselves. The following incident is concerned
with two of the Indians who had been captured by Kieft's soldiers
because of the accusations: The braves had been turned over to the
soldiers, by Kieft, to do with as they pleased.

The first of these savages, having received a frightful wound,
desired them to permit him to dance the Kinte Kaye, a religious use
among them before death; he received, however, so many wounds
that he dropped dead. The soldiers then cut strips down the other's
body. . . . While this was going forward Director Kieft, with his
Councillor (the first trained physician in the colony) Jan de la
Montagne, a Frenchman, stood laughing heartily at the fun, and
rubbing his right arm, so much delight he took in such scenes. He
then ordered him (the brave) to be taken out of the fort, and the
soldiers bringing him to the Beaver's Path, he dancing the Kinte
Kaye all the time, mutilated him, and at last cut off his head.

There stood at the same time, 24 or 25 female savages, who had
been taken prisoners, at the north-west corner of the fort: they held
up their arms, and in their language exclaimed, "For shame! for
shame! such unheard of cruelty was never known, or even thought
of, among us."

They made money of sea-shells. Bird feathers. Beaver skins. When
a priest died and was buried they encased him with such wealth as
he possessed. The Dutch dug up the body, stole the furs and left the
carcass to the wolves that roamed the woods.

                    Doc, listen — fiftyish, a grimy hand
                    pushing back the cap: In gold —
                              Volunteers of America

102

                                            I got
        a woman outside I want to marry, will
        you give her a blood test?

From 1869 to 1879 several crossed the falls on a tight rope (in the
old pictures the crowd, below, on the dry rocks in their short sleeves
and summer dresses look more like water-lilies or penguins than men
and women staring up at them): De Lave, Harry Leslie and Geo.
Dobbs—the last carrying a boy upon his shoulders. Fleetwood Miles,
a semi-lunatic, announced that he too would perform the feat but
could not be found when the crowd had assembled.

        The place sweats of staleness and of rot
        a back-house stench   .   a
        library stench

        It is summer!   stinking summer

        Escape from it—but not by running
        away. Not by "composition." Embrace the
        foulness

                    —the being taut, balanced between
        eternities

A spectator on Morris Mountain, when Leslie had gone out with
a cookstove strapped to his back—tugged at one of the guy-ropes,
either out of malice or idleness, so that he almost fell off. Having
carried the stove to the center of the rope he kindled a fire in it,
cooked an omelet and ate it. It rained that night so that the later
performance had to be postponed.

But on Monday he did the Washerwoman's Frolic, in female attire,
staggering drunkenly across the chasm, going backward, hopping on
one foot and at the rope's center lay down on his side. He retired
after that having "busted" his tights—to the cottage above for re-
pairs.

The progress of the events was transmitted over the new telephone
to the city from the tower of the water works. The boy, Tommy
Walker, was the real hero of these adventures.

And as reverie gains and
    your joints loosen
      the trick's done!
Day is covered and we see you—
      but not alone!
drunk and bedraggled to release

the strictness of beauty
under a sky full of stars
    Beautiful thing
and a slow moon —
           The car
    had stopped long since
    when the others
came and dragged those out
    who had you there
    indifferent
to whatever the anesthetic
    Beautiful Thing
might slum away the bars—

Reek of it!
    What does it matter?
    could set free
only the one thing—

But you!
—in your white lace dress

     •   •   •

    Haunted by your beauty (I said),
exalted and not easily to be attained, the
whole scene is haunted:
                Take off your clothes,
(I said)
    Haunted, the quietness of your face
is a quietness, real

out of no book.

Your clothes (I said) quickly, while
your beauty is attainable.

        Put them on the chair
(I said. Then in a fury, for which I am
ashamed)
        You smell as though you need
a bath. Take off your clothes and purify
yourself   . .
And let me purify myself
               —to look at you,
           to look at you (I said)

(Then, my anger rising)   TAKE OFF YOUR
CLOTHES ! I didn't ask you
to take off your skin . I said your
clothes, your clothes. You smell
like a whore. I ask you to bathe in my
opinions, the astonishing virtue of your
lost body (I said)   .

               —that you might
send me hurtling to the moon
. . let me look at you (I
said, weeping)

Let's take a ride around, to see what the town looks like

    Indifferent, the indifference of certain death
or incident upon certain death
propounds a riddle (in the Joyceian mode —
                  or otherwise,
it is indifferent which)
          A marriage riddle:

So much talk of the language—when there are no
ears.

. . . .

What is there to say? save that
beauty is unheeded . tho' for sale and
bought glibly enough

                    But it is true, they fear
it more than death, beauty is feared
more than death, more than they fear death

                              Beautiful thing

—and marry only to destroy, in private, in
their privacy only to destroy, to hide
                              (in marriage)
that they may destroy and not be perceived
in it—the destroying

Death will be too late to bring us aid .

What end but love, that stares death in the eye?
A city, a marriage — that stares death
in the eye

The riddle of a man and a woman

For what is there but love, that stares death
in the eye, love, begetting marriage —
not infamy, not death

                    tho' love seem to beget
only death in the old plays, only death, it is
as tho' they wished death rather than to face
infamy, the infamy of old cities .

.   .   .   a world of corrupt cities,
nothing else, that death stares in the eye,
lacking love: no palaces, no secluded gardens,
no water among the stones; the stone rails
of the balustrades, scooped out, running with
clear water, no peace   .

                              The waters
are dry. It is summer, it is   .   ended

Sing me a song to make death tolerable, a song
of a man and a woman: the riddle of a man
and a woman.
              What language could allay our thirsts,
what winds lift us, what floods bear us
                              past defeats
but song but deathless song ?

              The rock
              married to the river
              makes
              no sound

              And the river
              passes—but I remain
              clamant
              calling out ceaselessly
              to the birds
              and clouds
(listening)
              Who am I?

                              —the voice!

—the voice rises, neglected
(with its new) the unfaltering
language. Is there no release?

Give it up. Quit it. Stop writing.
"Saintlike" you will never
separate that stain of sense,

                an offense
to love, the mind's worm eating
out the core, unappeased

—never separate that stain
of sense from the inert mass.   Never.
Never that radiance

             quartered apart,
unapproached by symbols   .

Doctor, do you believe in
"the people," the Democracy? Do
you still believe — in this
swill-hole of corrupt cities?
Do you, Doctor?   Now?

             Give up
the poem. Give up the shilly-
shally of art.

           What can you, what
can YOU hope to conclude —
on a heap of dirty linen?

              — you
a poet (ridded) from Paradise?

Is it a dirty book? I'll bet
it's a dirty book, she said.

        Death lies in wait,
a kindly brother —
full of the missing words,
the words that never get said—
a kindly brother to the poor.
The radiant gist that
resists the final crystallization

    .   in the pitch-blend
the radiant gist   .

There was an earlier day, of prismatic colors : whence
to New Barbadoes came the Englishman   .

                        Thus it began .

Certainly there is no mystery to the fact
that Costs Spiral According to a Rebus—known
or unknown, plotted or automatic. The fact
of poverty is not a matter of argument. Language
is not a vague province. There is a poetry
of the movements of cost, known or unknown .

The cost. The cost

        and dazzled half sleepy eyes
                Beautiful thing
        of some trusting animal
                makes a temple
        of its place of savage slaughter
        .   .   .   .   .   .

        Try another book. Break through
        the dry air of the place

An insane god
      —nights in a brothel
      And if I had .
What then?

—made brothels my home?
      (Toulouse Lautrec
      again. .)

Say I am the locus
      where two women meet

One from the backwoods
      a touch of the savage
      and of T.B.
      (a scar on the thigh)
The other — wanting,
      from an old culture .
—and offer the same dish
      different ways

Let the colors run .

Toulouse Lautrec witnessed
it: limbs relaxed
—all religions
      have excluded it—
at ease, the tendons
untensed .

And so he recorded them

—a stone
thrust flint-blue
up through the sandstone
of which, broken,
      but unbreakable
we build our roads .

      —we stammer and elect   .

Quit it.   Quit this place.   Go where all
mouths are rinsed : to the river for
an answer
          for relief from "meaning"

A tornado approaches (We don't have
tornados in these latitudes. What, at
Cherry Hill?)

                       It pours
over the roofs of Paterson, ripping,
twisting, tortuous   :

a wooden shingle driven half its length
into an oak
          (the wind must have steeled
it, held it hard on both sides)

                    The church
moved 8 inches through an arc, on its
foundations —

          Hum, hum!

             —the wind
where it poured its heavy plaits (the face
unshowing) from the rock's edge —

          where in the updraft,
summer days, the red-shouldered hawks ride
and play
          (in the up-draft)

                    and the poor cotton-
spinner, over the roofs, preparing to dive
        .   looks down
Searching among books; the mind elsewhere
looking down

                    Seeking.

Fire burns; that is the first law.
When a wind fans it the flames

are carried abroad. Talk
fans the flames. They have

manoeuvred it so that to write
is a fire and not only of the blood.

The writing is nothing, the being
in a position to write (that's

where they get you) is nine tenths
of the difficulty: seduction

or strong arm stuff. The writing
should be a relief,

relief from the conditions
which as we advance become — a fire,

a destroying fire. For the writing
is also an attack and means must be

found to scotch it — at the root
if possible. So that

to write, nine tenths of the problem
is to live. They see

to it, not by intellection but
by sub-intellection (to want to be

blind as a pretext for
saying, We're so proud of you!

A wonderful gift! How *do*
you find the time for it in

your busy life? It must be a great
thing to have such a pastime.

But you were always a strange
boy. How's your mother?)

—the cyclonic fury, the fire,
the leaden flood and finally
the cost—

Your father was *such* a nice man.
I remember him well   .

Or, Geeze, Doc, I guess it's all right
but what the hell does it mean?

With due ceremony a hut would be constructed consisting of
twelve poles, each of a different species of wood. These they run
into the ground, tie them together at the top, cover them entirely
with bark, skins or blankets joined close together.   .   Now here
is where one sits who will address the Spirit of Fire, He-Who-Lies-
With-His-Eyes-Bulging-In-The-Smoke-Hole   .   Twelve
manittos attend him as subordinate deities, half representing animals
and the others vegetables. A large oven is built in the house of sacri-
fice   .   heated with twelve large red-hot stones.

Meanwhile an old man throws twelve pipefuls of tobacco upon the
hot stones, and directly another follows and pours water on them,
which occasions a smoke or vapor almost powerful enough to
suffocate the persons in the tent   —

Ex qua re, quia sicubi fumus adscendit in altum; ita sacrificulus,
duplicata altiori voce, *Kännakä, kännakä!* vel aliquando *Hoo Hoo!*
faciem versus orientem convertit.

Whereupon as the smoke ascends on high, the sacrificer crying
with a loud voice, *Kännakä, Kännakä!* or sometimes *Hoo, Hoo!*
turns his face towards the east.

While some are silent during the sacrifice, certain make a
ridiculous speech, while others imitate the cock, the squirrel and
other animals, and make all kinds of noises. During the shouting
two roast deer are distributed.

114

                    (breathing the books in)
the acrid fumes,
                    for what they could decipher   .
warping the sense to detect the norm, to break
through the skull of custom
                            to a place hidden from
affection, women and offspring — an affection
for the burning   .

It started in the car barns of the street railway company, in the
paint shop. The men had been working all day refinishing old cars
with the doors and windows kept closed because of the weather
which was very cold. There was paint and especially varnish being
used freely on all sides. Heaps of paint soaked rags had been thrown
into the corners. One of the cars took fire in the night.

Breathless and in haste
the various night (of books) awakes! awakes
and begins (a second time) its song, pending the
obloquy of dawn   .
                    It will not last forever
against the long sea, the long, long
sea, swept by winds, the "wine-dark sea"   .

A cyclotron, a sifting   .

            And there,
in the tobacco hush : in a tepee they lie
huddled (a huddle of books)
                    antagonistic,
                            and dream of
gentleness—under the malignity of the hush
they cannot penetrate and cannot waken, to be again
active but remain—books
                    that is, men in hell,
their reign over the living ended

115

Clearly, they say. Oh clearly! Clearly?
What more clear than that of all things
nothing is so unclear, between man and
his writing, as to which is the man and
which the thing and of them both which
is the more to be valued

When discovered it was a small blaze, though it was hot but it
looked as tho' the firemen could handle it. But at dawn a wind came
up and the flames (which they thought were subsiding) got suddenly
out of control—sweeping the block and heading toward the business
district. Before noon the whole city was doomed —

                Beautiful thing
                      —the whole city doomed! And
the flames towering   .

                    like a mouse, like
                    a red slipper, like
                    a star, a geranium,
                    a cat's tongue or —

                    thought, thought
                    that is a leaf, a
                    pebble, an old man
                    out of a story by

                    Pushkin   .

                              Ah!
                  rotten beams tum-
                  bling,

                       .   an old bottle
mauled

The night was made day by the flames, flames
on which he fed—grubbing the page
                              (the burning page)
like a worm—for enlightenment

Of which we drink and are drunk and in the end
are destroyed (as we feed). But the flames
are flames with a requirement, a belly of their
own that destroys—as there are fires that
smolder
        smolder a lifetime and never burst
into flame

                                              Papers
      (consumed) scattered to the winds. Black.
      The ink burned white, metal white. So be it.
      Come overall beauty. Come soon. So be it.
      A dust between the fingers. So be it.
      Come tatterdemalion futility. Win through.
      So be it.   So be it.

              An iron dog, eyes
aflame in a flame-filled corridor. A drunkenness
of flames. So be it. A bottle, mauled
by the flames, belly-bent with laughter:
yellow, green. So be it—of drunkenness
survived, in guffaws of flame. All fire afire!
So be it. Swallowing the fire. So be
it. Torqued to laughter by the fire,
the very fire. So be it. Chortling at flames
sucked in, a multiformity of laughter, a
flaming gravity surpassing the sobriety of
flames, a chastity of annihilation. Recreant,
calling it good. Calling the fire good.
So be it. The beauty of fire-blasted sand
that was glass, that was a bottle: unbottled.
Unabashed.   So be it.

An old bottle, mauled by the fire
gets a new glaze, the glass warped
to a new distinction, reclaiming the
undefined. A hot stone, reached
by the tide, crackled over by fine
lines, the glaze unspoiled   .
Annihilation ameliorated: Hottest
lips lifted till no shape but a vast
molt of the news flows. Drink
of the news, fluid to the breath.
Shouts its laughter, crying out—by
an investment of grace in the sand
—or stone: oasis water. The glass
splotched with concentric rainbows
of cold fire that the fire has bequeathed
there as it cools, its flame
defied—the flame that wrapped the glass
deflowered, reflowered there by
the flame: a second flame, surpassing
heat   .

Hell's fire.   Fire.   Sit your horny ass
down. What's your game? Beat you
at your own game, Fire. Outlast you:
Poet Beats Fire at Its Own Game! The bottle!
the bottle! the bottle! the bottle! I
give you the bottle! What's burning
now, Fire?

The Library?

                Whirling flames, leaping
from house to house, building to building

                        carried by the wind

the Library is in their path

Beautiful thing! aflame   .

                        a defiance of authority
—burnt Sappho's poems, burned
by intention (or are they still hid
in the Vatican crypts?)   :
                        beauty is
a defiance of authority   :

                        for they were
unwrapped, fragment by fragment, from
outer mummy cases of papier mâché inside
Egyptian sarcophagi   .

                        flying papers
from old conflagrations, picked up
haphazard by the undertakers to make
moulds, layer after layer
                        for the dead

Beautiful thing

The anthology suppressed, revived even by
the dead, you who understand nothing
of this:

        Dürer's *Melancholy*, the gears
lying disrelated to the mathematics of the
machine

        Useless.

                Beautiful thing, your
vulgarity of beauty surpasses all their
perfections!

Vulgarity surpasses all perfections
—it leaps from a varnish pot and we see
it pass — in flames!

Beautiful thing

—intertwined with the fire. An identity
surmounting the world, its core — from which
we shrink squirting little hoses of
                              objection — and
I along with the rest, squirting
at the fire

Poet.
                    Are you there?

How shall I find examples? Some boy
who drove a bull-dozer through
the barrage at Iwo Jima and turned it
and drove back making a path for the others —

                         Voiceless, his
action gracing a flame
                         —but lost, lost
because there is no way to link
the syllables anew to imprison him

             No twist of the flame
in his own image : he goes nameless
until a Niké shall live in his honor —

And for that, invention is lacking,
the words are lacking:

                   the waterfall of the
flames, a cataract reversed, shooting
upward (what difference does it make?)

The language,

           Beautiful thing—that I
make a fool of myself, mourning the lack
of dedication

           mourning its losses,
for you

        Scarred, fire swept
(by a nameless fire, that is unknown even
to yourself) nameless,

              drunk.

Rising, with a whirling motion, the person
passed into the flame, becomes the flame—
the flame taking over the person

            —with a roar, an outcry
which none can afford (we die in silence, we
enjoy shamefacedly—in silence, hiding
our joy even from each other
               keeping
a secret joy in the flame which we dare
not acknowledge)

           a shriek of fire with
the upwind, whirling the room away—to reveal
the awesome sight of a tin roof (1880)
entire, half a block long, lifted like a
skirt, held by the fire—to rise at last,
almost with a sigh, rise and float, float
upon the flames as upon a sweet breeze,
and majestically drift off, riding the air,
           sliding

upon the air, easily and away over
the frizzled elms that seem to bend under
it, clearing the railroad tracks to fall
upon the roofs beyond, red hot
darkening the rooms

                        (but not our minds)

While we stand with our mouths open,
shaking our heads and saying, My God, did
you ever see anything like that? As though
it were wholly out of our dreams, as
indeed it is, unparalleled in our most sanguine
dreams   .

                  The person submerged
in wonder, the fire become the person   .

But the pathetic library (that contained,
perhaps, not one volume of distinction)
must go down also —

            BECAUSE IT IS SILENT. IT
IS SILENT BY DEFECT OF VIRTUE IN THAT IT
CONTAINS NOTHING OF YOU

                  That which should be
rare is trash; because it contains
nothing of you. They spit on you,
literally, but without you, nothing. The
library is muffled and dead

                But you are the dream
of dead men

                  Beautiful Thing!

Let them explain you and you will be
the heart of the explanation. Nameless,
you will appear

                         Beautiful Thing
the flame's lover —

                      The pitiful dead
cry back to us from the fire, cold in
the fire, crying out—wanting to be chaffed
and cherished
                  those who have written books

      We read: not the flames
      but the ruin left
      by the conflagration

      Not the enormous burning
      but the dead (the books
      remaining). Let us read   .

      and digest: the surface
      glistens, only the surface.
      Dig in—and you have

      a nothing, surrounded by
      a surface, an inverted
      bell resounding, a

      white-hot man become
      a book, the emptiness of
      a cavern resounding

Hi Kid

    I know you just about to shot me. But honest Hon. I have
really been to busy to write. Here there, and everywhere.

    Bab I haven't wrote since October so I will go back to Oct. 31,
(Oh by the way are friend Madam B. Harris had a party the 31, but
only high browns and *yellow* so I wasn't invited)

But I pay that no mind, cause I really (pitched myself a ball)
Went to the show early in the day, and then to the dance at the
club. had me a (some kinded fine time) I was feeling good believe
me you. child.

But, child, Nov 1, I did crack you know yourself I been going
full force on the (jug) will we went out (going to Newark) was
raining, car slapped on brakes, car turned around a few times, rocked
a bit and stopped facing the other way, from which we was going.
Pal, believe me for the next few days. Honey, I couldn't even pick
up a half filled bucket of hot water for fear of scalding myself.

Now I don't know which did it the jug or the car skidding but
all I know is I was nowhere on nerves. But as they say alls well that
ends well   So Nov 15, I mean Kid I was so teaed that I didn't know
a from z I really mean I was teaed   Since Nov 15 I Have been at
it again ever since.

But now for the (Boys)   How Raymond James People going
with Sis but is in jail for giving Joseble Miller a baby.

Robert Blocker has taken his ring from Sally Mitchell

Little Sonny Jones is supposed to be the father of a girl's baby
on Liberty St.

Sally Mund Barbara H Jean C and Mary M are all supposed to
be going to have kids Nelson W. a boy on 3rd St is father to 3 kids
on their way.

.   .   .   .

P. S.   Kid do you think in your next letter of your you could tell
me how to get over there.

Tell Raymond I said   I bubetut hatche isus cashutute
Just a new way of talking kid. It is called (Tut) maybe you heard
of it. Well here hoping you can read it

D
J
B

So long.

Later

Beautiful thing

I saw you:

Yes, said

the Lady of the House to my questioning.
Downstairs

(by the laundry tubs)

and she pointed,

124

smiling, to the basement, still smiling, and
went out and left me with you (alone in the house)
lying there, ill
                    (I don't at all think that you
were ill)
            by the wall on your damp bed, your long
body stretched out negligently on the dirty sheet   .

Where is the pain?
                    (You put on a simper designed
not to reveal)

                —the small window with two panes,
my eye level of the ground, the furnace odor   .

                                Persephone
gone to hell, that hell could not keep with
the advancing season of pity.

                    —for I was overcome
by amazement and could do nothing but admire
and lean to care for you in your quietness —

who looked at me, smiling, and we remained
thus looking, each at the other   .   in silence   .

You lethargic, waiting upon me, waiting for
the fire and I
            attendant upon you, shaken by your beauty

Shaken by your beauty   .
                                Shaken.

— flat on your back, in a low bed (waiting)
under the mud plashed windows among the scabrous
dirt of the holy sheets   .

You showed me your legs, scarred (as a child)
by the whip   .

Read.   Bring the mind back (attendant upon
the page) to the day's heat. The page also is
the same beauty : a dry beauty of the page —
beaten by whips

                    A tapestry hound
with his thread teeth drawing crimson from
the throat of the unicorn

        .   .   .   a yelping of white hounds
— under a ceiling like that of San Lorenzo, the long
painted beams, straight across, that preceded
the domes and arches
                    more primitive, square edged

        .   a docile queen, not bothered
to stick her tongue out at the moon, indifferent,
through loss, but   .

                    queenly,
in bad luck, the luck of the stars, the black stars

                .   the night of a mine

Dear heart
                It's all for you, my dove, my
                                    changeling

            But you!
            —in your white lace dress
                "the dying swan"
            and high-heeled slippers—tall
            as you already were—
                    till your head

through fruitful exaggeration
was reaching the sky and the
prickles of its ecstasy
    Beautiful Thing!
And the guys from Paterson
    beat up
the guys from Newark and told
them to stay the hell out
of their territory and then
socked you one
    across the nose
    Beautiful Thing
for good luck and emphasis
    cracking it
till I must believe that all
desired women have had each
    in the end
    a busted nose
and live afterward marked up
    Beautiful Thing
    for memory's sake
to be credible in their deeds

Then back to the party!
    and they maled
and femaled you jealously
    Beautiful Thing
as if to discover whence and
    by what miracle
there should escape, what?
still to be possessed, out of
    what part
    Beautiful Thing
should it look?
    or be extinguished—
Three days in the same dress
    up and down   .

I can't be half gentle enough,
half tender enough
                toward you, toward you,
inarticulate, not half loving enough

BRIGHTen
                the cor
                                ner
where   you   are!

                        —a flame,
        black plush, a dark flame.

III

It is dangerous to leave written that which is badly written. A chance word, upon paper, may destroy the world. Watch carefully and erase, while the power is still yours, I say to myself, for all that is put down, once it escapes, may rot its way into a thousand minds, the corn become a black smut, and all libraries, of necessity, be burned to the ground as a consequence.

Only one answer: write carelessly so that nothing that is not green will survive.

> There is a drumming of submerged
> engines, a beat of propellers.
> The ears are water. The feet
> listen. Boney fish bearing lights
> stalk the eyes — which float about,
> indifferent. A taste of iodine
> stagnates upon the law of percent-
> ages: thick boards bored through
> by worms whose calcined husks
> cut our fingers, which bleed   .

We walk into a dream, from certainty to the unascertained, in time to see   .   from the roseate past   .   a ribbed tail deploying

> Tra la la la la la la la la
> La tra tra tra tra tra tra

> Upon which there intervenes
> a sour stench of embers. So be it. Rain
> falls and surfeits the river's upper reaches,
> gathering slowly. So be it. Draws together,
> runnel by runnel. So be it. A broken oar
> is found by the searching waters. Loosened

129

it begins to move. So be it. Old timbers
sigh—and yield. The well that gave sweet water
is sullied. So be it. And lilies that floated
quiet in the shallows, anchored, tug as
fish at a line. So be it. And are by their
stems pulled under, drowned in the muddy flux.
The white crane flies into the wood.
So be it. Men stand at the bridge, silent,
watching. So be it. So be it.

                         And there rises
a counterpart, of reading, slowly, overwhelming
the mind; anchors him in his chair. So be
it. He turns   .   O Paradiso! The stream
grows leaden within him, his lilies drag. So
be it. Texts mount and complicate them-
selves, lead to further texts and those
to synopses, digests and emendations. So be it.
Until the words break loose or—sadly
hold, unshaken. Unshaken! So be it. For
the made-arch holds, the water piles up debris
against it but it is unshaken. They gather
upon the bridge and look down, unshaken.
So be it. So be it. So be it.

   The sullen, leaden flood, the silken flood
   —to the teeth

                 to the very eyes

                         (light grey)

Henry's the name. Just Henry,
                        ever'body
knows me around here: hat
pulled down hard on his skull, thick chested,
fiftyish   .

                  I'll hold the baby.

That was your little dog bit me last year.
Yeah, and you had him killed on me.

(the eyes)

I didn't know he'd been killed.

You reported him and
they come and took him. He never hurt
anybody.
He bit me three times.
They come and
took him and killed him.
I'm sorry but I had
to. report him   .   .

A dog, head dropped back, under water, legs
sticking up   :
a skin
tense with the wine of death
downstream
on the swift current   :
Above the silence
a faint hissing, a seething hardly at first
to be noticed

—headlong!

Speed!

—marked
as by the lines on slate, mottled by petty
whirlpools

(to the teeth, to the very eyes)

a formal progression

The remains—a man of gigantic stature—were transported on the shoulders of the most renowned warriors of the surrounding country .   for many hours they travelled without rest. But half way on the journey the carriers had to quit overcome by fatigue— they had walked many hours and Pogatticut was heavy. So by the side of the trail, at a place called "Whooping Boys Hollow," they scooped out a shallow hole and laid the dead chieftain down in it while they rested. By so doing, the spot became sacred, held in veneration by the Indians.

Arrived at the burial place the funeral procession was met by Pogatticut's brothers and their followers. There was great lamentation and the Kinte Kaye was performed in sadness.

Wyandach, the most illustrious brother, performed the burial sacrifice. Having his favorite dog, a much loved animal, brought forth, he killed him, and laid him, after painting his muzzle red, beside his brother. For three days and three nights the tribes mourned   .

> Pursued by the whirlpool-mouths, the dog
> descends toward Acheron   .   Le Néant
>   .   the sewer   .
>   a dead dog
>
>   turning
> upon the water:
>
>
>   Come yeah, Chi Chi!
>
>
>   turning
> as he passes   .
>
>
> It is a sort of chant, a sort of praise, a
> peace that comes of destruction:
>   to the teeth,
> to the very eyes
>
>   (cut lead)

<pre>   I bin nipped
hundreds of times. He never done anybody any
harm   .
                helpless   .

            You had him killed on me.
</pre>

About Merselis Van Giesen a curious story illustrative of the superstition of the day is to this effect: His wife was ill for a long time, confined to her bed. As she lay there, a black cat would come, night after night, and stare at her through the window, with wicked, blazing eyes. An uncanny fact about this visitation was that *no one else could see the cat*. That Jane was bewitched was the belief of the whole neighborhood. Moreover, the witch who exercised this spell, and who made these weird visits to the sufferer, in the guise of a cat invisible to everybody but the bewitched, was believed to be Mrs. B. who lived in the gorge in the hill beyond.

Happy souls! whose devils lived so near.

Talking the matter over with his neighbors, Merselis (he was called "Sale") was told that if he could shoot the spectral cat with a silver bullet he would kill the creature, and put a stop to the spells exercised over his wife. He did not have a silver bullet, but he had a pair of silver sleeve buttons.

Who of us thinks so fast to switch the category
of our loves and hatreds?

Loading his gun with one of these buttons, he seated himself on the bed beside his wife, and declared his intention of shooting the witch cat. But how could he shoot a creature he could not see?

Are we any better off?

"When the cat comes," said he to his wife, "do you point out just where it is, and I will shoot at that spot." So they waited, she in a tremor of hope and dread—hope that the spells afflicting her would soon be ended; dread that some new torment might come to her from this daring attempt of her husband; he, in grim determination to forever end the unholy power exercised over his wife by Mrs. B., in the guise of the invisible feline. Long and silently they waited.

133

—what a picture of marital fidelity! dreaming as one.

At last, when their feelings had been wrought up, by the suspense to the highest pitch, Jane exclaimed "There is the black cat!" "Where?" "At the window, it's walking on the sill, it is in the lower left-hand corner!" Quick as a flash "Sale" raised his gun and fired the silver bullet at the black cat which he could not see. With a snarl that was a scream the mysterious creature vanished forever from the gaze of Mrs. Van Giesen, who from that hour began to recover her health.

The next day "Sale" started out on a hunt through what is now known as Cedar Cliff Park. On the way he met the husband of the suspected witch. There was the usual exchange of courteous neighborly inquiries regarding the health of their respective families. Mr. B. said his wife was troubled with a sore on her leg for some time. "I would like to see that sore leg," said "Sale." After some demur he was taken to the house, and on one plea or another was finally permitted to examine the sore. But what particularly attracted his notice was a fresh wound, just where his silver sleeve button had struck the unfortunate creature when she had last visited his wife in the form of the spectral black witch cat! Needless to say Mrs. B. never more made those weird visitations. Perhaps it was from a sense of thanksgiving for her miraculous deliverance that Mrs. Van Giesen joined the First Presbyterian Church on Confession, Sept. 26, 1823. Merselis Van Giesen was assessed in 1807 for 62 acres of unimproved land, two horses and five cattle.

     — 62 acres of unimproved land, two horses
and five cattle —

       (that cures the fantasy)

             The Book of Lead,
he cannot lift the pages

         (Why do I bother with this
rubbish?)

134

                              Heavy plaits
tumbling massive, yellow into the cleft,
bellowing

                —giving way to the spread
of the flood as it lifts to recognition in a
rachitic brain

        (the water two feet now on the turnpike
and still rising)

                    There is no ease.
                    We close our eyes,
                    get what we use
                    and pay. He owes
                    who cannot, double.
                    Use. Ask no whys?
                    None wants our ayes.

But somehow a man must lift himself
again —
                again is the magic word   .
                        turning the in out   :
Speed against the inundation

He feels he ought to *do* more. He had
a young girl there. Her mother told her,
Go jump off the falls, who cares? —
She was only fifteen. He feels so frustrated.
I tell him, What do you expect, you
have only two hands   .   ?

It was a place to see, she said, The White Shutters. He said I'd
be perfectly safe there with him. But I never went. I wanted to, I
wasn't afraid but it just never happened. He had a small orchestra

135

that played there, *The Clipper Crew* he called it—like in all the speakeasies of those days. But one night they came leaping down-stairs from the banquet hall tearing their clothes off, the women throwing their skirts over their heads, and joined in the dancing, naked, with the others on the main floor. He took one look and then went out the back window just ahead of the police, in his dress shoes into the mud along the river bank.

Let me see, Puerto Plata is
the port of Santo Domingo.

There was a time when
they didn't want any whites
to own anything—to
hold anything—to say, This
is mine   .

I see things,   .   .

—the water at this stage no lullaby but a piston,
cohabitous, scouring the stones   .

the rock
floating on the water (as at Mt Katmai
the pumice-covered sea was white as milk)

One can imagine
the fish hiding or
at full speed
stationary
in the leaping stream

—it's undermining the railroad embankment

Hi, open up a dozen, make
it two dozen!   Easy girl!

You wanna blow a fuse?

All manner of particularizations
to stay the pocky moon   :
                                January sunshine   .
                        1949
Wednesday, 11
                (10,000,000 times plus April)
—a red-butted reversible minute-glass

            loaded with
salt-like   white crystals
            flowing

                for timing eggs

Salut à Antonin Artaud pour les

    lignes, trés pures   :

        "*et d'évocations plas-
        tiques d'éléments de*"

                            and
"Funeral *designs*"
            (a beautiful, optimistic
word   .   .   )   and
        "Plants"
                    (it should be explained that
in this case "plants" does NOT refer to interment.)

    "Wedding bouquets"
                —the association
is indefensible.

(re. C.O.E.   Panda Panda   )

Fer gor Zake/ don't so egggzaggerate/
I never told you to *read* it.
let erlone REread it.   I didn't
say it *wuz ! ! henjoyable* readin.
I sd/ the guy had done some honest
work devilupping his theatre technique

———————————

That don't necess/y mean making
reading matter @ all.
Enny how there must be
one hundred books (*not*
that one) that you *need* to
read fer yr/ mind's sake.

———————————

re read *all* the Gk tragedies in
Loeb.—plus Frobenius, plus
Gesell   plus Brooks Adams
ef you ain't read him all. —
Then Golding 'Ovid' is in Everyman lib.

———————————

& nif you want a readin
list ask papa—but don't
go rushin to *read* a book
just cause it is mentioned eng
passang. is fraugs. . . .

SUBSTRATUM

Artesian well at the Passaic Rolling Mill, Paterson.

The following is the tabular account of the specimens found in this well, with the depths at which they were taken, in feet. The boring began in September, 1879, and was continued until November, 1880.

DEPTH	DESCRIPTION OF MATERIALS
65 feet. . .	Red sandstone, fine
110 feet. . .	Red sandstone, coarse
182 feet. . .	Red sandstone, and a little shale
400 feet. . .	Red sandstone, shaly
404 feet. . .	Shale
430 feet. . .	Red sandstone, fine grained
540 feet. . .	Sandy shale, soft
565 feet. . .	Soft shale
585 feet. . .	Soft shale
600 feet. . .	Hard sandstone
605 feet. . .	Soft shale
609 feet. . .	Soft shale
1,170 feet. . .	Selenite, 2 x 1 $\frac{1}{16}$ in.
1,180 feet. . .	Fine quicksand, reddish
1,180 feet. . .	Pyrites
1,370 feet. . .	Sandy rock, under quicksand
1,400 feet. . .	Dark red sandstone
1,400 feet. . .	Light red sandstone
1,415 feet. . .	Dark red sandstone
1,415 feet. . .	Light red sandstone
1,415 feet. . .	Fragments of red sandstone
1,540 feet. . .	Red sandstone, and a pebble of kaolin
1,700 feet. . .	Light red sandstone
1,830 feet. . .	Light red sandstone
1,830 feet. . .	Light red sandstone
1,830 feet. . .	Light red stone
2,000 feet. . .	Red shale
2,020 feet. . .	Light red sandstone
2,050 feet. . .	
2,100 feet. . .	Shaly sandstone

At this depth the attempt to bore through the red sandstone was abandoned, the water being altogether unfit for ordinary use. . . . The fact that the rock salt of England, and of some of the other salt mines of Europe, is found in rocks of the same age as this, raises the question whether it may not also be found here.

```
                — to the teeth, to the very eyes
        .    uh,    uh

                    FULL STOP

                —and leave the world
                    to darkness
                    and to
                        me
```

When the water has receded most things have lost their
form. They lean in the direction the current went. Mud
covers them

                    —fertile(?)mud.

If it were only fertile. Rather a sort of muck, a detritus,
in this case—a pustular scum, a decay, a choking
lifelessness—that leaves the soil clogged after it,
that glues the sandy bottom and blackens stones—so that
they have to be scoured three times when, because of
an attractive brokenness, we take them up for garden uses.
An acrid, a revolting stench comes out of them, almost one
might say a granular stench—fouls the mind   .

How to begin to find a shape—to begin to begin again,
turning the inside out : to find one phrase that will
lie married beside another for delight   .   ?
—seems beyond attainment   .

American poetry is a very easy subject to discuss for the
simple reason that it does not exist

                Degraded. The leaf torn from
                the calendar. All forgot. Give
                it over to the woman, let her
                begin again—with insects
                and decay, decay and then insects :
                the leaves—that were varnished

140

with sediment, fallen, the clutter
made piecemeal by decay, a
digestion takes place   .

—of this, make it of *this*, this
this, this, this, this   .

Where the dredge dumped the fill,
something, a white hop-clover
with cordy roots (of iron) gripped
the sand in its claws—and blossomed
massively, where the old farm
was and the man broke his wife's
cancerous jaw because she was
too weak, too sick, that is, to
work in the field for him as he
thought she should   .

So thinking, he composed
a song to her:
     to entertain her
in her reading:

          *   *   *

The birds in winter
and in summer the flowers
those are her two joys
—to cover her secret sorrow

Love is her sorrow
over which at heart
she cries for joy by the hour
—a secret she will not reveal

Her ohs are ahs
her ahs are ohs
and her sad joys
fly with the birds and blossom
                with the rose

— the edema subsides

Who is it spoke of April? Some
insane engineer. There is no recurrence.
The past is dead. Women are
legalists, they want to rescue
a framework of laws, a skeleton of
practices, a calcined reticulum
of the past which, bees, they will
fill with honey   .

It is not to be done. The seepage has
rotted out the curtain. The mesh
is decayed. Loosen the flesh
from the machine, build no more
bridges. Through what air will you
fly to span the continents? Let the words
fall any way at all—that they may
hit love aslant. It will be a rare
visitation. They want to rescue too much,
the flood has done its work

Go down, peer among the fishes. What
do you expect to save, muscle shells?

Here's a fossil conch (a paper weight
of sufficient quaintness) mud
and shells baked by a near eternity
into a melange, hard as stone, full of
tiny shells
—baked by endless desiccations into

a shelly rime—turned up
in an old pasture whose history—
even whose partial history, is
death itself

                  Vercingetorix, the only
hero   .

Let's give the canary to that
old deaf woman; when he opens his
bill, to hiss at her, she'll think he
is singing   .

Does the pulp need further maceration?
take down the walls, invite
the trespass. After all, the slums
unless they are (living)
wiped out they cannot be re-
constituted   .

The words will have to be rebricked up, the
—what? What am I coming to   .
                        pouring down?

When an African Ibibio man is slain in battle, married women
who are his next of kin rescue the corpse. No man may touch it.
Weeping and singing songs, the scouts bear the dead warrior to
a forest glade called Owokafai—the place of those slain by sudden
death. They lay him on a bed made of fresh leaves. Then they cut
young branches from a sacred tree and wave the bough over the
genital organs of the warrior to extract the spirit of fertility into
the leaves. Knowledge of the rites must be kept from men and
from unmarried girls. Only married women, who have felt the
fertility of men in their bodies, can know the secret of life. To
them it was entrusted by their great goddess "in the days when
woman, not man, was the dominant sex. . ; on the guarding of
this secret depended the strength of the tribe. Were the rites once
disclosed—few or no babies would be born, barns and herds would
yield but scanty increase, while the arms of future generations of

143

fighting men would lose their strength and hearts their courage."
This ceremony is conducted to the accompaniment of low, wailing
chants, which only these wives of warriors have authority to sing,
or even to know.

       —in a hundred years, perhaps—
       the syllables
              (with genius)
                     or perhaps
     two lifetimes

     Sometimes it takes longer   .

Did I do more than share your guilt, sweet woman. The
cherimoya is the most delicately flavored of all
tropic fruit.   .   .   Either I abandon you
or give up writing   .

I was thinking about her all day long yesterday. You know she's
been dead four years? And that son of a bitch only has one more
year to serve. Then he'll be out and we can't do a thing about it. —
I suppose he killed her. — You *know* he killed her, just shot her to
death. And do you remember that Clifford that used to follow her
around, poor man? He'd do anything she asked him to—the most
harmless creature in the world; he's been sick. He had rheumatic
fever when he was a child and can't leave the house any more. He
wrote to us to send him some dirty jokes because he can't get out
to hear them himself. And we can't either of us think of one new
one to send him.

     The past above, the future below
     and the present pouring down: the roar,
     the roar of the present, a speech—
     is, of necessity, my sole concern   .

     They plunged, they fell in a swoon   .
     or by intention, to make an end—the
     roar, unrelenting, witnessing   .
     Neither the past nor the future

Neither to stare, amnesic—forgetting.
The language cascades into the
invisible, beyond and above : the falls
of which it is the visible part —

Not until I have made of it a replica
will my sins be forgiven and my
disease cured—in wax: *la capella di S. Rocco*
on the sandstone crest above the old

copper mines—where I used to see
the images of arms and knees
hung on nails (de Montpellier) .
No meaning. And yet, unless I find a place

apart from it, I am its slave,
its sleeper, bewildered—dazzled
by distance   .   I cannot stay here
to spend my life looking into the past:

the future's no answer. I must
find my meaning and lay it, white,
beside the sliding water: myself —
comb out the language—or succumb

—whatever the complexion. Let
me out!   (Well, go!) this rhetoric
is real!

Book Four

The Run to the Sea

I

An Idyl

Corydon & Phyllis

Two silly women!

                   (Look, Dad, I'm dancing!)

What's that?

             I didn't say anything .
except *you* don't look silly   .

Semantics, my dear .

             — and I know *I'm* not   .

Ouch! you have hands like a man . Some day,
sweetheart, when we know each other better
I'll tell you a few things . .
Thank you. Very satisfactory. My secretary
will be at the door with your money   .
No. I prefer it that way

          O. K.

                 Good-bye
Miss . eh

         Phyllis

149

Tiens!   I'll phone the agency   .
Until tomorrow, then, Phyllis, at the same hour.
Shall I be walking again soon, do you think?

Why not?

.   .   .   .   .   .

A Letter

Look, Big Shot, I refuse to come home until you promise to cut
out the booze. It's no use your talking about Mother needs
me and all that bologney. If you thought anything of her you
wouldn't carry on the way you do. Maybe your family did
once own the whole valley. Who owns it now? What you
need is to be slapped down.

I'm having a fine time in the Big City as a Professional Woman,
ahem! Believe me there's plenty of money here — if you can
get it. With your brains and ability this should be your meat.
But you'd rather hit the bottle.

That's all right with me — only I won't wrestle with you all
night on the bed any more because you got the D.Ts. I can't
take it, your too strong for me. So make up your mind — one
way or the other.

.   .   .   .   .   .

Corydon & Phyllis

And how are you today, darling?

(She calls me darling now!)

What sort of life can you lead
in that horrid place   .   Rach-a-mo, did
you say?

150

        Ramapo
                To be sure,
how stupid of me.

        Right.

              What was that?
Really you'll have to speak louder

        I said   .

            Never mind.

You mentioned a city?

        Paterson, where I trained

           Paterson!
Yes, of course. Where Nicholas Murray Butler was
born   . and his sister, the lame one. They
used to have silk mills there   .
until the unions ruined them. Too bad.   Wonderful
hands! I completely forget myself   .
Some hands are silver, some gold and some,
a very few, like yours, diamonds (If only I
could keep you!) You like it here?   .   Go
look out of that window   .

That is the East River. The sun rises there.
And beyond, is Blackwell's Island. Welfare Island,
City Island   . whatever they call it now   .
where the city's petty criminals, the poor
the superannuated and the insane are housed   .

Look at me when I talk to you

                                        — and then
the three rocks tapering off into the water   .
all that's left of the elemental, the primitive
in this environment.   I call them my sheep   .

                    Sheep, huh?

Docile, are they not?

                    What's the idea?

Lonesomeness perhaps. It's a long story. Be
their shepherdess Phyllis. And I
shall be Corydon   .   inoffensively, I hope?
Phyllis and Corydon.   How lovely!   Do you
care for almonds?

                              Nope. I hate all kinds of
nuts.   They get in your hair   .   your
teeth, I mean   .

    .   .   .   .   .

A Letter

Lay off that stuff. I can take care of myself. And if not, so
what?

This is a racket, all I got to do is give her "massage" — and
what do I know about massage? I just rub her, and how I rub
her! And does she like it! And does she pay! Oh boy! So I
rub her and read to her. The place is full of books—in all
languages!

But she's a nut, of the worst kind. Today she was telling me
about some rocks in the river here she calls her three sheep. If
they're sheep I'm the Queen of England. They're white all
right but it's from the gulls that crap them up all day long.

152

You ought to see this place.

There was a hellicopter (?) flying all over the river today looking for the body of a suicide, some student, some girl about my age (she says . a Hindu Princess). It was in the papers this morning but I didn't take notice. You ought to have seen the way those gulls were winging it around. They went crazy .

•   •   •   •   •   •

Corydon & Phyllis

You must have lots of boy friends, Phyllis

                    Only one

Incredible!

                    Only one I'm interested in
right now

What is he like?

                    Who?

Your lover

                    Oh him.   He's married. I
haven't got a chance with him

You hussy!   And what do you do together?

                    Just talk.

•   •   •   •   •   •

Phyllis & Paterson

                    Are you happy?
            Happy I've come?

            Happy?   No, I'm not happy

                    Never?

            Well   .

                    The couch looks
            comfortable

    .   .   .   .   .   .

The Poet

        Oh Paterson!   Oh married man!
        He is the city of cheap hotels and private
        entrances   .   of taxis at the door, the car
        standing in the rain hour after hour by
        the roadhouse entrance   .

        Good-bye, dear. I had a wonderful time.
        Wait! there's something   .   but I've forgotten
        what it was   .   something I wanted
        to tell you. Completely gone!   Completely.
        Well, good-bye   .

    .   .   .   .   .   .

Phyllis & Paterson

            How long can you stay?

            Six-thirty   .   I've got
            to meet the boy friend

Take off your clothes

No. I'm good at saying that.

She stood
quietly to be undressed   .

the buttons were difficult   .
This is one of my father's
best. You ought to have heard
him this morning when I
cut the tails off   .

He drew back the white
shirt   .   slid aside the
ribbons   .

Glory be to God   .

— then stripped her

and all His Saints!

.

No, just broad shouldered

.

— on the couch, kissing and talking while his
hands explored her body, slowly   .
courteously   .   persistent   .

.

Be careful   .
I've got an awful cold

It's the first
this year. We went
fishing in all
that rain last week

Who?   Your father?
— and my boy friend

Fly fishing?
No. Bass. But it isn't

the season. I know that
but nobody saw us

I got soaked to the skin
Can you fish?

Oh I have a pole and a
line and just fish along

We caught quite a few

   .   .   .   .   .   .

Corydon & Phyllis

   Good morning, Phyllis. You are beautiful this morning
(in a common sort of way) I wonder if you know how
lovely you really are, Phyllis, my little Milk Maid   (That's
good! The lucky man!) I dreamt of you last night.

A Letter

I don't care what you say. Unless Mother writes me, herself, that you've stopped drinking — and I mean *stopped drinking* — I won't come home.

.

Corydon & Phyllis

What sort of people do you come from, Phyllis?

My father's a drunk.
That's more humility than the situation demands. Never be ashamed of your origins.

I'm not. It's just the truth.

The truth!   Virtue, my dear, if one had it! is only interesting in the aggregate, as you will discover . or perhaps you have already found it so. That's our Christian teaching: not denial but forgiveness, the Prodigal Daughter. Have you ever been to bed with a man?

Have you?

Good shot! With this body? I think I'm more horse than woman. Did you ever see such skin as mine? Speckled like a Guinea hen   .

Only *their* speckles are white.

More like a toad, perhaps?

I didn't say that.

Why not? It's the truth, my little Oread. In-
domitable. Let's change names. You be Corydon! And I'll
play Phyllis. Young! Innocent! One can fairly hear the pelt-
ing of apples and the stomp and clatter of Pan's hoofbeats.
Tantamount to nothing   .

.   .   .   .   .   .

Phyllis & Paterson

Look at us!   Why do you
torment yourself?
You think I'm a virgin.
Suppose I told you
I'd had intercourse. What
would you say then?
What would you say? Suppose
I told you that   .

She leaned forward in
the half light, close to
his face.   Tell
me, what would you say?

Have you had many lovers?

No one who has mauled me
the way you have. Look,
we're all sweaty   .

.

My father's trying to get me a horse   .

.

I went out, once, with a boy
I only knew him a short time

He asked me   .   .
No, I said, of course not!

He acted so surprised.
Why, he said, most girls

are crazy for it. I
thought they all were   .

You ought to have seen
my eyes.   I never heard
of such a thing   .

                         .

      I don't know why I can't give myself to you. A man
like you should have everything he wants   .   I guess I care
too much, that's the trouble   .

.   .   .   .   .   .

Corydon & Phyllis

      Phyllis, good morning. Could you stand a drink at
this early hour? I've written you a poem   .   and the worst
is, I'm about to read it to you   .   You don't have to like it.
But, hell take it, you damn well better listen to it. Look at
me shake! Or better, let me give you a short one, to begin
with:

If I am virtuous
condemn me
If my life is felicitous
condemn me
The world is
iniquitous

Mean anything?

Not much.

Well, here's another:

You dreamy
          Communist
where are you
          going?

To world's end
          Via?
Chemistry
          Oh oh oh oh

That will
          really
be the end   .
          you

dreamy Communist
          won't it?
Together
          together

"With that she split her girdle." Gimme another shot.
I always fell on my face when I wanted to step out. But here
goes! Here it is. This is what I've been leading up to. It's
called, *Corydon, a Pastoral.* We'll skip the first part, about the
rocks and sheep, begin with the helicopter. You remember
that?

>   .   .   drives the gulls up in a cloud
> Um .   no more woods and fields.   Therefore
> present, forever present

>   .   a whirring pterodactyl
> of a contrivance, to remind one of Da Vinci,
> searches the Hellgate current for some corpse,
> lest the gulls feed on it
> and its identity and its sex, *as* its hopes, and its
> despairs and its moles and its marks and
> its teeth and its nails be no longer decipherable
> and so lost   .
>   therefore present,
>   forever present   .
> The gulls, vortices of despair, circle and give
> voice to their wild responses until the thing
> is gone   .   then, ravening, having scattered
> to survive, close again upon the focus,
> the bare stones, three harbor stones, except
> for that   .   useless
>   unprofaned   .

It stinks!

>   If this were rhyme, Sweetheart
>   such rhyme as might be made
>   jaws would hang open   .

But the measure of it is the thing   .   None
             can wish for an embellishment
and keep his mind lean,
             fit for action   .
such action as I plan

             — to turn my hand up and hold
it open, to the rain   .
             of their deaths
that I brood   .   and find none ready
             but mine own   .

Nuts! After that, how about a story that's a little   .
recherché, a little strong? To hide my embarrassment?
O.K.?

Sure.

Skip it.

             A ring is round
             but cannot bind
             though it may bound
             a lover's mind

                          Phyllis, I think I'm
quite well now   .   .   How would you like to go
fishing with me somewhere?   You like to fish   .

Can I bring my father?

No, you can't bring your father. You're a big girl now.
A month with me, in the woods! I have a concession. Don't
answer at once. You've never been to Anticosti   .   ?

What's it like, pizza?

Phyllis, you're a bad girl. Let me go on with my poem

.   .   .   .   .   .

Dear Pappy:

How yuh doin'? Are you behaving? because she wants me to go fishing with her. For a month! What do you say? You'd like that.

.

Is that so? Well, you know where you can get off at. And don't think you can start coming in here. Because if you do I'll *never* go home. And you *haven't stopped drinking!* Don't try to kid me.

.

Alright, if you think I'm in danger then learn to behave yourself. Are you a weakling or something? But I won't go through all that again. Never. Don't worry, as I told you, I can take care of myself. And if anything happens to me, so what? Blame it on I've got a father who is a drunk.

Your daughter
P.

.   .   .   .   .   .

Phyllis & Paterson

> This dress is sweaty. I'll have
> to have it cleaned
> It lifted past the shoulders.
> Under it, her stockings
>
> Big thighs   .
>
> Let us read, said the King
> lightly. Let us

                    redivagate, said the Queen
                    even more lightly

                    and without batting an eye

                                     .

                    He took her nipples
                    gently in his lips. No
                    I don't like it

    .   .   .   .   .   .

Corydon & Phyllis

        You remember where we left off? At the entrance to the
45th Street tunnel   .   Let's see

                              .   houses placarded:
        Unfit for human habitation   etc   etc

Oh yes   .

                                        Condemned   .
        But who has been condemned   .   where the tunnel
        under the river starts? *Voi ch'entrate*
        revisited!   Under ground, under rock, under river
        under gulls   .   under the insane   .

        .   the traffic is engulfed and disappears   .
        to emerge   .   never

        A voice calling in the hubbub (Why else
        are there newspapers, by the cart-load?) blaring
        the news no wit shall evade, no rhyme
        cover. Necessity gripping the words   .   scouting
        evasion, that love is begrimed, befouled   .

164

I'd like to spill the truth, on that one.

Why don't you?

This is a POEM!

                              begrimed
yet lifts its head, having suffered a sea-change!
shorn of its eyes and its hair
its teeth kicked out   .   a bitter submersion
in darkness   .   a gelding, not to be
listed   .   to be made ready! fit to
serve (vermin trout, that eat the salmon eggs,
gaze up through the dazzle   .   in glass
necklaces   .   picturesque peasant stuff
without value)   .   pulp

                    While in the tall
buildings (sliding up and down) is where
the money's made
                    up and down
                              directed missiles
in the greased shafts of the tall buildings   .
They stand torpid in cages, in violent motion
unmoved
              but alert!
                         predatory minds, un-
affected
              UNINCONVENIENCED
                         unsexed, up
and down (without wing motion) This is how
the money's made   .   using such plugs.

                                              At the
sanitary lunch hour packed woman to
woman (or man to woman, what's the difference?)
the flesh of their faces gone
to fat or gristle, without recognizable
outline, fixed in rigors, adipose or sclerosis
expressionless, facing one another, a mould
for all faces (canned fish) this   .

Move toward the back, please, and face the door!

is how the money's made,
                          money's made
                                        pressed together
talking excitedly   .   of the next sandwich   .
reading, from one hand, of some student, come
waterlogged to the surface following
last night's thunderstorm   .   the flesh a
flesh of tears and fighting gulls   .

                            Oh I could cry!
cry upon your young shoulder for what I know.
I feel so alone   .

     .   .   .   .   .   .

Phyllis & Paterson

                I think I'll go on the stage,
                said she, with a deprecating laugh,
                Ho, ho!

                Why don't you? he replied
                though the legs, I'm afraid, would
                beat you   .

166

.   with me, Phyllis
(I'm no Simaetha) in all your native loveliness
that these spiked rumors may not tear
                              that sweet flesh

It sounds as tho' I wanted to eat you, I'll have to change that.

Come with me to Anticosti, where the salmon
lie spawning in the sun in the shallow water

                    I think that's Yeats   .

— and we shall fish for the salmon fish

                    No, I think *that's* the Yeats   .

                         — and its silver
shall be our crest and guerdon (what's a guerdon?)
drawn struggling   .

                    Believe me, some tussle!

                    from the icy water   .

    I wish you'd come, dear, I've got my yacht all stocked
and ready. Let me take you on a tour   .   of Paradise!

    That I'd like to see.

    Then why not come?

    I'm not ready to die yet, not even for that.

    You don't need to.

Dear Pappy:

For the last time!

All day today, believe it or not, we've been coasting along what they call up here the North Shore on our way to the place we're going to fish at. It sounds like an Italian dinner, Anticosti, but it's really french.

It's wild, they say, but we have a marvellous guide, an Indian I think but it's not sure (maybe I'll marry him and stay up there for the rest of my life) Anyway he speaks french and the Missis talks to him in that language. I don't know what they're saying (and I don't care, I can talk my own language).

I can hardly keep my eyes open, I've been out almost every night this week. To go on. We have wine, mostly Champagne on board. She showed it to me, 24 cases for the party but I don't want any of it, thanks. I'll stick to my rum and coke. Don't worry. Tell Ma everything's all right. But remember, I'm through.

Phyllis & Paterson

Do you know that tall
dark girl with the long nose?
She's my friend.   She says
she's going West next fall.

I'm saving every cent I
can put together.   I'm going
with her.   I haven't told
my mother yet   .

Why do you torment yourself?   I can't
think unless you're naked.   I wouldn't blame

you if you beat me up, punched me,
anything at all . I wouldn't do

you that much honor. What! what did you say?
I said I wouldn't do you that much

honor .   So that's all?
I'm afraid so. Something I shall always

desire, you've seen to that. Talk to me.
This is not the time for it. Why did you let

me come? Who knows, why *did* you? I like
coming here, I need you. I know that .

hoping I'd take it from you, lacking
your consent. I've lost out, haven't I?

You have. Pull down my slip .
He lay upon his back upon the couch.

She came, half dressed, and straddled him.
My thighs are sore from riding .

Oh let me breathe! After I'm married
you must take me out sometime. If that's

what you want .

Corydon & Phyllis

Have any of these men
you speak of . ?
— and has he?

No.

Good.

What's good about it?

Then you're still a virgin!

What's it to *you?*

II

You were not more than 12, my son
                14 perhaps, the high school age
when we went, together,
             a first for both of us,
to a lecture, in the Solarium
             topping the hospital, on atomic
fission. I hoped to discover
             an "interest" on your part.
You listened   .

           Smash the world, wide!
           — if I could do it for you —
           Smash the wide world   .
           a fetid womb, a sump!
           No river! no river
           but bog, a   .   swale
           sinks into the mind or
           the mind into it, a   ?

Norman Douglas (*South Wind*) said to me, The best thing a
man can do for his son, when he is born, is to die   .

    I gave you another, bigger than yourself, to contend with.

    To resume:

(What I miss, said your mother, is the poetry, the pure poem
of the first parts   .)

    The moon was in its first quarter.
             As we approached the hospital
the air above it, having taken up
             the glow through the glass roof
seemed ablaze, rivalling night's queen.

The room was packed with doctors.
How pale and young the boy seemed
                    among those pigs, myself
among them! who surpassed him
                    only in experience, that drug,
sitting erect to their talk:
                    valences   .

For years a nurse-girl
                    an unhatched sun corroding
her mind, eating away a rind
                    of impermanences, through books
remorseless   .

Curie (the movie queen) upon
                    the stage at the Sorbonne   .
a half mile across!   walking solitary
                    as tho' in a forest, the silence
of a great forest (of ideas)
                    before the assembly (the
little Polish baby-nurse) receives
                    international acclaim (a
drug)

            Come on up! Come up Sister and be
        saved (splitting the atom of
        bitterness)!   And Billy Sunday evangel
        and ex-rightfielder sets himself
        to take one off the wall   .

                                        He's *on*
        the table now!   Both feet, singing
        (a foot song) his feet canonized   .

                            .   as paid for
        by the United Factory Owners' Ass'n   .

.   to "break" the strike
and put those S.O.Bs in their places, be
Geezus, by calling them to God!

— getting his 27 Grand in the hotel room
after the last supper (at the *Hamilton*)
on the eve of quitting town, exhausted
in his efforts to split (a split
personality)   .   the plate

What an arm!

Come to Jesus!   .   Someone help
that old woman up the steps   .   Come to
Jesus and be   .   All together now,
give it everything you got!

Brighten
.   .   the corner where you
are!

Dear Doctor:
   In spite of the grey secrecy of time and my own self-shuttering
doubts in these youthful rainy days, I would like to make my pres-
ence in Paterson known to you, and I hope you will welcome this
from me, an unknown young poet, to you, an unknown old poet,
who live in the same rusty county of the world. Not only do I
inscribe this missive somewhat in the style of those courteous sages
of yore who recognized one another across the generations as
brotherly children of the muses (whose names they well know)
but also as fellow citizenly Chinamen of the same province, whose
gastanks, junkyards, fens of the alley, millways, funeral parlors,
river-visions—aye! the falls itself—are images white-woven in their
very beards.
   I went to see you once briefly two years ago (when I was 21),
to interview you for a local newspaper. I wrote the story in fine
and simple style, but it was hacked and changed and came out the
next week as a labored joke at your expense which I assume you
did not get to see. You invited me politely to return, but I did not,

as I had nothing to talk about except images of cloudy light, and was not able to speak to you in your own or my own concrete terms. Which failing still hangs with me to a lesser extent, yet I feel ready to approach you once more.

As to my history: I went to Columbia on and off since 1943, working and travelling around the country and aboard ships when I was not in school, studying English. I won a few poetry prizes there and edited the Columbia Review. I liked Van Doren most there. I worked later on the Associated Press as a copyboy, and spent most of the last year in a mental hospital; and now I am back in Paterson which is home for the first time in seven years. What I'll do there I don't know yet—my first move was to try and get a job on one of the newspapers here and in Passaic, but that hasn't been successful yet.

My literary liking is Melville in Pierre and the Confidence Man, and in my own generation, one Jack Kerouac whose first book came out this year.

I do not know if you will like my poetry or not—that is, how far your own inventive persistence excludes less independent or youthful attempts to perfect, renew, transfigure, and make contemporarily real an old style of lyric machinery, which I use to record the struggle with imagination of the clouds, with which I have been concerned. I enclose a few samples of my best writing. All that I have done has a program, consciously or not, running on from phase to phase, from the beginnings of emotional breakdown, to momentary raindrops from the clouds become corporeal, to a renewal of human objectivity which I take to be ultimately identical with no ideas but in things. But this last development I have yet to turn into poetic reality. I envision for myself some kind of new speech—different at least from what I have been writing down—in that it has to be clear statement of fact about misery (and not misery itself), and splendor if there is any out of the subjective wanderings through Paterson. This place is as I say my natural habitat by memory, and I am not following in your traces to be poetic: though I know you will be pleased to realize that at least one actual citizen of your community has inherited your experience in his struggle to love and know his own world-city, through your work, which is an accomplishment you almost cannot have hoped to achieve. It is misery I see (like a tide out of my own fantasy) but mainly the splendor which I carry within me and which all free men do. But harking back to a few sentences previous, I may need a new measure myself, but though I have a flair for your style I seldom dig exactly what you are doing with cadences, line length, sometimes syntax, etc., and cannot handle your work as a solid object—which properties I assume you rightly claim. I don't understand the measure. I haven't worked with it much either, though, which must make the difference. But I would like to talk with you concretely on this.

I enclose these poems. The first shows you where I was 2 years ago. The second, a kind of dense lyric I instinctively try to imitate—after Crane, Robinson, Tate, and old Englishmen. Then, the Shroudy Stranger (3) less interesting as a poem (or less sincere) but it connects observations of *things* with an old dream of the void—I have real dreams about a classic hooded figure. But this dream has become identified with my own abyss—and with the abyss of old Smokies under the Erie R.R. tracks on straight street —so the shroudy stranger (4) speaking from the inside of the old wracked bum of Paterson or anywhere in America. This is only a half made poem (using a few lines and a situation I had in a dream). I contemplated a long work on the shroudy stranger, his wanderings. Next (5) an earlier poem, Radio City, a long lyric written in sickness. Then a mad song (to be sung by Groucho Marx to a Bop background.) (6). The (7) an old style ballad-type ghost dream poem. Then, an ode to the Setting Sun of abstract (8) ideas, written before leaving the hospital, and last an Ode to Judgment, which I just wrote, but which is unfinished. (9) What will come of all this I do not know yet.

I know this letter finds you in good health, as I saw you speak at the Museum in N. Y. this week. I ran backstage to accost you, but changed my mind, after waving at you, and ran off again.

Respectfully yours,
A. G.

Paris, a fifth floor room, bread
milk and chocolate, a few
apples and coal to be carried,
des briquettes, their special smell,
at dawn: Paris   .
the soft coal smell, as she
leaned upon the window before de-
parting, for work   .

—a furnace, a cavity aching
toward fission; a hollow,
a woman waiting to be filled

—a luminosity of elements, the
current leaping!
Pitchblende from Austria, the
valence of Uranium inexplicably
increased. Curie, the man, gave up
his work to buttress her.

But she is pregnant!
                    Poor Joseph,

the Italians say.

Glory to God in the highest
and on earth, peace, goodwill to
men!

Believe it or not.

    A dissonance
    in the valence of Uranium
    led to the discovery

    Dissonance
    (if you are interested)
    leads to discovery

    —to dissect away
    the block and leave
    a separate metal:

    hydrogen
    the flame, helium the
    pregnant ash   .

—the elephant takes two years

Love is a kitten, a pleasant
thing, a purr and a
pounce. Chases a piece of
string, a scratch and a mew
a ball batted with a paw   .
a sheathed claw   .

Love, the sledge that smashes the atom?   No, No! antagonistic
cooperation is the key, says Levy   .

Sir Thopas (The Canterbury Pilgrims) says (to Chaucer)
            Namoor—
            Thy drasty rymyng is not
            worth a toord
—and Chaucer seemed to think so too for he stopped and went
on in prose   .

Report of Cases

CASE 1.—M. N., a white woman aged 35, a nurse in the pediatric
ward, had no history of previous intestinal disturbance. A sister
who lived with her suffered with cramps and diarrhea, later found
by us to be due to amebiasis. On Nov. 8, 1944 a stool submitted by
the nurse for the usual monthly examination was found to be posi-
tive for Salmonella montevideo. The nurse was at once removed
from duty with full pay, a measure found to be of advantage in
having hospital personnel report diarrheal disturbances without
fear of economic reprisal.

            —with ponderous belly, full
            of thought!   stirring the cauldrons
            .   in the old shed used
            by the medical students for dissections.
            Winter.   Snow through the cracks

177

                              Pauvre étudiant   .
             en l'an trentième de mon âge
             Item   .   with coarsened hands
             by the hour, the day, the week
             to get, after months of labor   .

             a stain at the bottom of the retort
             without weight, a failure, a
             nothing.   And then, returning in the
             night, to find it   .

LUMINOUS!

   On Friday, the twelfth of October, we anchored before the
land and made ready to go ashore   .   There I sent the people
for water, some with arms, and others with casks: and as it was
some little distance, I waited two hours for them.
   During that time I walked among the trees which was the
most beautiful thing which I had ever known.

         .   knowledge, the contaminant

             Uranium, the complex atom, breaking
             down, a city in itself, that complex
             atom, always breaking down   .
             to lead.
                      But giving off that, to an
             exposed plate, will reveal   .

             And so, with coarsened hands
                                      she stirs

             And love, bitterly contesting, waits
             that the mind shall declare itself not
             alone in dreams   .

   A man like you should have everything he wants   .

178

                    not half asleep
waiting for the sun to part the labia
of shabby clouds . but a man (or
a woman) achieved

                            flagrant!
adept at thought, playing the words
following a table which is the synthesis
of thought, a symbol that is to him,
sun up! a Mendelief, the elements laid
out by molecular weight, identity
predicted before found! and   .

Oh most powerful connective, a bead
to lie between continents through
which a string passes   .

Ah Madam!
this is order, perfect and controlled
on which empires, alas, are built

But there may issue, a contaminant,
some other metal radioactive
a dissonance, unless the table lie,
may cure the cancer   .   must
lie in that ash . Helium plus, plus
what? Never mind, but plus   .   a
woman, a small Polish baby-nurse
unable .

Woman is the weaker vessel, but
the mind is neutral, a bead linking
continents, brow and toe

and will at best take out
its spate in mathematics
                    replacing murder

Sappho vs Elektra!

The young conductor gets his orchestra
and leaves his patroness
                    with child.

.   *les idées Wilsoniennes nous
gâtent*   .   the vague irrelevances
and the destructive silences
                            inertia

As Carrie Nation
          to Artemis
                so is our life today   .

They took her out West on a photographing
expedition
            to study chiaroscuro
                        to Denver, I think.
Somewhere around there   .
                                the marriage
was annulled. When she returned
                        with the baby
                                openly
taking it to her girls' parties, they
                            were shocked

— and the Abbess Hildegard, at her own
funeral, Rupertsberg, 1179
had enjoined them to sing the choral, all
women, she had written for the occasion
and it was done, the peasants kneeling
in the background   .   as you may see

The Constitution says: *To borrow money on the credit of the United States.* It does not say: To borrow money from Private bankers.

To explain the fallacies and illusions upon which our present method of financing the national budget is based would take too much space and time. To win the cold war we must reform our finance system. The Russians understand only force. We must be stronger than they and build more airplanes.

FINANCE THE BUILDING OF AIRPLANES AS FOLLOWS:

1. Pay the manufacturer with a NATIONAL CREDIT CERTIFICATE.
2. Manufacturer deposits the Certificate with his bank the same as a check.
3. Banker returns National Credit Certificate to Treasury Dept., which opens UNITED STATES NATIONAL CREDIT for banker.
4. Banker in turn now opens BANKER'S CREDIT for depositor. Manufacturer draws checks against his credit as usual.
5. Manufacturer pays his workers with checks upon his bank.
6. Treasury Dept. pays banker a service charge of 1% for handling the Treasury transaction. If the airplanes cost 1 million dollars the banker's profit would be $10,000.

WHAT DO WE ACCOMPLISH BY USING THIS SYSTEM?

1. Manufacturer is paid in full.
2. Workers are paid in full.
3. Bankers make a $10,000. profit every time he handles a 1 million dollar National Credit Certificate.
4. We do not add to the National Debt.
5. We do not have to increase federal taxation.
6. The only cost of the 1 million dollar airplane is only $10,000, the cost of the banker's service charges.
7. We can build 100 airplanes for the price of one.

I would like to have some smart economist or banker stick out his neck and contradict one single claim I present herewith to the nation.

ENFORCE THE CONSTITUTION ON MONEY

———

August Walters, Newark, N. J.

MONEY : JOKE (i.e., crime
        under the circumstances : value
        chipped away at accelerated pace.)

— do you joke when a man is dying
                        of a brain tumor?

Take up the individual misfortune
by buffering it into the locality — not
penalize him with surgeon's fees
and accessories at an advance over the
market price for

                "hospital income"

Who gets that?   The poor?
                        What poor?
— at $8.50 a day, ward rate?
        short of the possibility of recovery

And not enrich the widow either
                long past fertility

Money: Uranium (bound to be lead)
throws out the fire   .
— the radium's the credit — the wind in
the trees, the hurricane in the
palm trees, the tornado that lifts
oceans   .
Trade winds that broached a continent
drive the ship forward   .

Money sequestered enriches avarice, makes
poverty: the direct cause of
disaster   .
                while the leak drips
Let out the fire, let the wind go!
Release the Gamma rays that cure the cancer

.   the cancer, usury. Let credit
out   .   out from between the bars
before the bank windows

          .   credit, stalled
in money, conceals the generative
that thwarts art or buys it (without
understanding), out of poverty of wit, to
win, vicariously, the blue ribbon

                              to win
the Congressional Medal
for bravery beyond the call of duty but
not to end as a bridge-tender
on government dole   .

                         Defeat may steel us
in knowledge : money : joke
to be wiped out sooner or later at stroke
of pen   .

.   just because they ain't no water fit to drink in that spot (or
you ain't found none) don't mean there ain't no fresh water to
be had NOWHERE   .   .

          — and to Tolson and to his ode
          and to Liberia and to Allen Tate
          (Give him credit)
          and to the South generally
                    Selah!

          — and to 100 years of it — splits
          off the radium, the Gamma rays
          will eat their bastard bones out who
          are opposed
                    Selah!

Pobres bastardos, misquierdos
             Pobrecitos
       Ay!   que pobres

— yuh wanna be killed with your
face in the dirt and a son-of-a-bitch
of a *Guardia Civil* giving you the
             coup de (dis)grace
right in the puss   .   ?

             Selah!   Selah!

Credit!   I hope you have a long credit
       and a dirty one
             Selah!

What is credit?   the Parthenon

What is money?   the gold entrusted to Phideas for the
                    statue of Pallas Athena, that he "put aside"
                    for private purposes

       — the gold, in short, that Phideas stole
You can't steal credit :   the Parthenon.

— let's skip any reference, at this time, to the Elgin marbles.

             Reuther — shot through a window, at whose pay?

— then there's Ben Shahn   .

             Here follows a list of the mayors of
             120 American cities in the years following
             the Civil War.   .   or the War Between
             the States, if you prefer   .   like
             cubes of fat in the *blutwurst* of the
             times   .

Credit.   Credit.   Credit.   Give them all credit. They were
the fathers of many a later novelist no worse than the rest.

> Money : Joke
> could be wiped out
> at stroke
> of pen
> and was when
> gold and pound were
> devalued

> Money : small time
>   reciprocal action relic
> precedent to stream-lined
>   turbine : credit

> Uranium : basic thought — leadward
>   Fractured : radium : credit

> Curie : woman (of no importance) genius : radium

> THE GIST

> credit : the gist

IN
   venshun.
O.KAY
       In venshun

and seeinz az how yu hv/started.   Will you consider
a remedy of a lot :
                 i.e. LOCAL control of local purchasing
                                          power
                                          ? ?

185

Difference between squalor of spreading slums
and splendor of renaissance cities.

Credit makes solid
is related directly to the effort,
work: value created and received,
"the radiant gist" against all that
scants our lives.

Haven't you forgot your virgin purpose,
the language?

What language? "The past is for those who
lived in the past," is all she told me.

Shh!   the old man's asleep

—all but for the tides, there is no river,
silent now, twists and turns
in his dreams   .

                              The ocean yawns!
It is almost the hour

—and did you ever know of a sixty year
woman with child   .   ?

                         Listen!
someone's coming up the path,   .   perhaps
it is not too late?   Too late   .

JONATHAN, bap. Oct. 29, 1752; m. Gritie (Haring?). He was born
and brought up at Hoppertown (Hohokus), but in 1779 was run-
ning the grist and saw-mill at Wagaraw, now owned by the Alyeas.
On the night of April 21, 1779, his wife was aroused by a noise as
of someone trying to get into the lower part of the mill, where,
for better security, he kept his horses. "Yawntan," said she in
Dutch, "someone is stealing your horses." Lighting a lantern, he
threw open the upper half-door and challenged the marauders. In-
stantly a shot was fired through the lower half-door, wounding him
in the abdomen. He staggered back into the house and fell upon a
bed, covering himself up in the blankets. A party of Tories, masked
and disguised, rushed in, and, compelling his young wife to hold
a candle, they savagely attacked the prostrate form. Once he seized
one of the bayonettes and holding it for a moment, cried at his as-

187

sailant: "Andries, this is an old grudge." With redoubled fury the inhuman savages bayonetted him, until with a groan he expired. His two infant children who were wont to sleep in a trundle bed beneath his, were horrified spectators of their father's massacre. After the murderers were gone, his wife and a neighbor took the blood out of the bed in double handfuls. The murdered man had received nineteen or twenty cruel bayonette thrusts. It was believed that some neighbor had led the Tories to the attack, less from political or pecuniary considerations than from motives of private revenge. Hopper was a captain in the Bergen County militia. One of his children was Albert, bap. Oct. 6, 1776. It is said that Jonathan's children removed to Cincinnati, and there attained some prominence.

Come on, get going. The tide's in

Leise, leise!   Lentement!   Che va piano,
va lontano!   Virtue,
my kitten, is a complex reward in all
languages, achieved slowly.

.   which reminds me of
an old friend, now gone   .

—while he was still
in the hotel business, a tall and rather beautiful young woman came to his desk one day to ask if there were any interesting books to be had on the premises. He, being interested in literature, as she knew, replied that his own apartment was full of them and that, though he couldn't leave at the moment — Here's my key, go up and help yourself.

She thanked him and
went off. He forgot all about her.

After lunch he too
went to his rooms not remembering until he was at the door that he had no key. But the door was unlatched and as he entered, a girl was lying naked on the bed. It startled him a little. So much so that all he could do was to remove his own clothes and lie beside her. Quite comfortable, he soon fell into a heavy sleep. She also must have slept.

They wakened later,
simultaneously, much refreshed.

188

                    —another, once gave me
an old ash-tray, a bit of
                    porcelain inscribed
with the legend, *La Vertue*
                    est toute dans l'effort
baked into the material,
                    maroon on white, a glazed
Venerian scallop   .   for
                    ashes, fit repository
for legend, a quieting thought:
                    Virtue is wholly
in the effort to be virtuous   .
                    This takes connivance,
takes convoluted forms, takes
                    time!   A sea-shell   .
Let's not dwell on childhood's
                    lecherous cousins.   Why
should we? Or even on
                    as comparatively simple
a thing as the composite
                    dandelion that
changes its face overnight   .   Virtue,
                    a mask: the mask,
virtuous   .

Kill the explicit sentence, don't you think? and expand our mean-
ing—by verbal sequences. Sentences, but not grammatical sen-
tences: dead-falls set by schoolmen. Do you think there is any
virtue in that? better than sleep? to revive us?

            She used to call me her
                    country bumpkin
            Now she is gone I think
                    of her as in Heaven
            She made me believe in
                    it   .   a little
            Where else could she go?

                                                    189

There was
Something grandiose
about her   .
Man and woman are not
much emphasized as
such at that age: both
want the same
thing   . to be amused.
Imagine *me*
at her funeral. I sat
way back.   Stupid,
perhaps but no more so
than any funeral.
You might think she had
a private ticket.
I think she did; some
people, not many,
make you feel that way.
It's in them.

Virtue, she would say   .
(her version of it)
is a stout old bird,
unpredictable.   And
so I remember her,
adding,
as she did, clumsily,
not being used to
such talk, that —
Nothing does, does
as it used to do
do do!   I loved her.

All the professions, all the arts,
idiots, criminals to the greatest
lack and deformity, the stable parts
making up a man's mind — fly
after him attacking ears and eyes:
small birds following marauding
crows, in ecstasies   .   of fear
and daring

The brain is weak.   It fails mastery,
never a fact.

          To bring himself in,
hold together wives in one wife and
at the same time scatter it,
the one in all of them   .
                    Weakness,
weakness dogs him, fulfillment only
a dream or in a dream. No one mind
can do it all, runs smooth
in the effort: *toute dans l'effort*

          The greyhaired President
(of Haiti), his women and children,
               at the water's edge,
sweating, leads off finally, after
delays, huzzahs, songs for pageant reasons
over the blue water   .
in a private plane
               with his blonde secretary.

Scattered, the fierceness
of knowledge comes flocking down again—

                    souvenir of childhood,
the skull of the white stone   .
There was Margaret of the big breasts
and daring eyes who carried
her head, where her small brain rattled,
as the mind might wish,
at the best, to be carried. There was
Lucille, gold hair and blue eyes, very
straight, who
to the amazement of many, married a
saloon keeper and lost her modesty.
There was loving Alma, who wrote a steady
hand, whose mouth never wished for
relief.   And the cold Nancy, with small
firm breasts   .

                    You remember?

                            .   a high
forehead, she who never smiled more
than was sufficient but whose broad
mouth was icy with pleasure startling
the back and knees!   whose words were
few and never wasted. There were
others — half hearted, the over-eager,
the dull, pity for all of them, staring
out of dirty windows, hopeless, indifferent,
come too late and a few, too drunk
with it — or anything — to be awake to
receive it.   All these
and more — shining, struggling flies
caught in the meshes of Her hair, of whom
there can be no complaint, fast in
the invisible net — from the back country,
half awakened — all desiring.   Not one
to escape, not one   .   a fragrance
of mown hay, facing the rapacious,
the "great"   .

The whereabouts of Peter the Dwarf's grave was unknown until the end of the last century, when, in 1885, P. Doremus, undertaker, was moving bodies from the cellar of the old church to make room for a new furnace, he disinterred a small coffin and beside it a large box. In the coffin was the headless skeleton of what he took to be a child until he opened the large box and found therein an enormous skull. In referring to the burial records it was learned that Peter the Dwarf had been so buried.

Yellow, for genius, the Jap said. Yellow
is your color. The sun. Everybody looked.
And you, purple, he added, wind over water.

My serpent, my river! genius of the fields,
Kra, my adored one, unspoiled by the mind,
observer of pigeons, rememberer of
cataracts, voluptuary of gulls!   Knower
of tides, counter of hours, wanings and
waxings, enumerator of snowflakes, starer
through thin ice, whose corpuscles are
minnows, whose drink, sand   .

Here's to the baby,
may it thrive!
Here's to the labia
that rive

to give it place
in a stubborn world.
And here's to the peak
from which the seed was hurled!

In a deep-set valley between hills, almost hid
by dense foliage lay the little village.
Dominated by the Falls the surrounding country
was a beautiful wilderness where mountain pink
and wood violet throve: a place inhabited only
by straggling trappers and wandering Indians.

A print in colors by Paul Sandby, a well known
water color artist of the eighteenth century,
a rare print in the Public Library
shows the old Falls restudied from a drawing
made by Lieut. Gov. Pownall (excellent work) as he
saw it in the year 1700.

The wigwam and the tomahawk, the Totowa tribe   .
On either side lay the river-farms resting in
the quiet of those colonial days: a hearty old
Dutch stock, with a toughness to stick and
hold fast, although not fast in making improvements.

Clothing homespun.   The people raised their own
stock. Rude furniture, sanded floors, rush
bottomed chair, a pewter shelf of Brittania
ware. The wives spun and wove — many things
that might appear disgraceful or distasteful today
The Benson and Doremus estates for years were
the only ones on the north side of the river.

Dear Doc: Since I last wrote I have settled down more, am working
on a Labor newspaper (N. J. Labor Herald, AFL) in Newark. The
owner is an Assemblyman and so I have a chance to see many of
the peripheral intimacies of political life which in this neighbor-
hood has always had for me the appeal of the rest of the land-
scape, and a little more, since it is the landscape alive and busy.

Do you know that the west side of City Hall, the street, is
nicknamed the Bourse, because of the continual political and bank-
ing haggle and hassel that goes on there?

Also I have been walking the streets and discovering the bars—
especially around the great Mill and River streets. Do you know
this part of Paterson? I have seen so many things—negroes, gypsies,
an incoherent bartender in a taproom overhanging the river, filled
with gas, ready to explode, the window facing the river painted
over so that the people can't see it. I wonder if you have seen
River Street most of all, because that is really at the heart of what
is to be known.

I keep wanting to write you a long letter about deep things I
can show you, and will some day—the look of streets and people,
events that have happened here and there.

A. G.

. . . .

There were colored slaves. In 1791 only ten
houses, all farm houses save one, The Godwin
Tavern, the most historic house in Paterson,
on River Street: a swinging sign on a high
post with a full length picture of Washington
painted on it, giving a squeaking sound when
touched by the wind.

Branching trees and ample gardens gave
the village streets a delightful charm and
the narrow old-fashioned brick walls added
a dignity to the shading trees. It was a fair
resort for summer sojourners on their way
to the Falls, the main object of interest.

The sun goes beyond Garrett Mountain
as evening descends, the green of its pine
trees, fading under a crimson sky until
all color is lost. In the town candle light
appears. No lighted streets. It is as dark
as Egypt.

There is the story of the cholera epidemic
the well known man who refused to bring his
team into town for fear of infecting them
but stopped beyond the river and carted his
produce in himself by wheelbarrow — to the
old market, in the Dutch style of those days.

Paterson, N. J., Sept. 17—Fred Goodell Jr., twenty-two, was arrested early this morning and charged with the murder of his six-months-old daughter Nancy, for whom police were looking since Tuesday, when Goodell reported her missing.

Continued questioning from last night until 1 a.m. by police headed by Chief James Walker drew the story of the slaying, police said, from the $40-a-week factory worker a few hours after he refused to join his wife, Marie, eighteen, in taking a lie detector test.

At 2 a.m. Goodell led police a few blocks from his house to a spot on Garrett Mountain and showed them a heavy rock under which he had buried Nancy, dressed only in a diaper and placed in a paper shopping bag.

Goodell told the police he had killed the child by twice snapping the wooden tray of a high chair into the baby's face Monday morning when her crying annoyed him as he was feeding her. Dr. George Surgent, the county physician, said she died of a fractured skull.

> There was an old wooden bridge to Manchester, as
> Totowa was called in those days, which
> Lafayette crossed in 1824, while little
> girls strewed flowers in his path. Just
> across the river in what is now called the Old
> Gun Mill Yard was a nail factory where
> they made nails by hand.

> I remember going down to the old cotton
> mill one morning when the thermometer was
> down to 13 degrees below on the old bell
> post. In those days there were few steam
> whistles. Most of the mills had a bell post
> and bell, to ring out the news, "Come to work!"

> Stepping out of bed into a snow drift
> that had sifted in through the roof; then,
> after a porridge breakfast, walk
> five miles to work. When I got there I
> did pound the anvil for sartin', to keep
> up circulation.

196

In the early days of Paterson, the breathing
spot of the village was the triangle square
bounded by Park Street (now lower Main St.)
and Bank Street. Not including the Falls it
was the prettiest spot in town. Well shaded
by trees with a common in the center where
the country circus pitched its tents.
On the Park Street side it ran down to
the river. On the Bank Street side it ran
to a roadway leading to the barnyard of
the Goodwin House, the barnyard taking up
part of the north side of the park.

The circus was an antiquated affair, only
a small tent, one ring show. They didn't
allow circuses to perform in the afternoon
because that would close up the mills. Time
in those days was precious. Only in the
evenings. But they were sure to parade their
horses about the town about the time the
mills stopped work. The upshot of the
matter was, the town turned out to the circus
in the evening. It was lighted

in those days by candles especially
made for the show. They were giants fastened
to boards hung on wires about the tent,
a peculiar contrivance. The giant candles
were placed on the bottom boards, and two
rows of smaller candles one above the other
tapering to a point, forming a very pretty
scene and giving plenty of light.

The candles lasted during the performance
presenting a weird but dazzling spectacle
in contrast with the showy performers —

Many of the old names and some of the
places are not remembered now: McCurdy's
Pond, Goffle Road, Boudinot Street. The
Town Clock Building. The old-fashioned
Dutch Church that burned down Dec. 14, 1871
as the clock was striking twelve midnight.
Collet, Carrick, Roswell Colt,
Dickerson, Ogden, Pennington   .   .
The part of town called Dublin
settled by the first Irish immigrants. If
you intended residing in the old town you'd
drink of the water of Dublin Spring. The
finest water he ever tasted, said Lafayette.

Just off Gun Mill yard, on the gully
was a long rustic winding stairs leading
to a cliff on the opposite side of the river.
At the top was Fyfield's tavern — watching
the birds flutter and bathe in the little
pools in the rocks formed by the falling
mist — of the Falls   .   .

Paterson, N. J., January 9, 1850:—The murder last night of
two persons living at the Goffle, within two or three miles of this
place has thrown our community into a state of intense excitement.
The victims are John S. Van Winkle and his wife, an aged couple,
and long residents of this county. The atrocious deed was accom-
plished as there appears no doubt by one John Johnson, a laboring
farmer, and who at the time was employed by some of his neigh-
bors in the same capacity. So far as we have been able to gather
the particulars, it would seem that Johnson effected an entrance
into the house through an upper window, by means of a ladder,
and descending to the bedroom of his victims below, accomplished
his murderous purpose by first attacking the wife who slept in
front, then the husband, and again the wife.

The second attack appears to have immediately deprived the
wife of life; the husband is still living but his death is momentarily
expected. The chief instrument used appears to have been a knife,
though the husband bears one or more marks of a hatchet. The

hatchet was found next morning either in bed or on the floor, and the knife on the window sill, where it was left by the murderer in descending to the ground.

A boy only slept in the same dwelling. . . . . The fresh snow, however, enabled his pursuers to find and arrest their man. . . . . His object was doubtless money (which, however, he seemed not to have obtained).

Johnson inquired why they had tied him, "what have I done?" , . . . He was taken to the scene of murder and shown the objects of his barbarous cruelty, but the sight produced no other sensible effect than to extort from him an expression of pity, he denying any knowledge of participation in the inhuman butchery.

> Trip a trap o'troontjes
> De vaarkens in de boontjes—
> De kocien in de klaver—
> De paarden in de haver—
> De eenden in de waterplas,
>   Plis! Plas!
> Zoo groot mijn kleine Derrick was!

You come today to see killed
                            killed, killed
as if it were a conclusion
                    —a conclusion!
a convincing strewing of corpses
—to move the mind

                as tho' the mind
can be moved, the mind, I said
by an array of hacked corpses:

                        War!
a poverty of resource   .   .

            Twenty feet of
guts on the black sands of Iwo

"What have I done?"

—to convince whom?   the sea worm?
They are used to death and
jubilate at it   .   .

Murder.

          —you cannot believe
that it can begin again, again, here
again   .   here
Waken from a dream, this dream of
the whole poem   .   sea-bound,
                    rises, a sea of blood

—the sea that sucks in all rivers,
                              dazzled, led
by the salmon and the shad   .

Turn back I warn you
                (October 10, 1950)
from the shark, that snaps
at his own trailing guts, makes a sunset
of the green water   .

But lullaby, they say, the time sea is
no more than sleep is   .   afloat
with weeds, bearing seeds   .

                          Ah!

float wrack, float words, snaring the
seeds   .

I warn you, the sea is *not* our home.
                    the sea is not our home

The sea *is* our home whither all rivers
(wither) run   .

                        the nostalgic sea
sopped with our cries
                    Thalassa! Thalassa!
calling us home   .
I say to you, Put wax rather in your
ears against the hungry sea
                        it is not our home!

.   draws us in to drown, of losses
and regrets   .

Oh that the rocks of the Areopagus had
kept their sounds, the voices of the law!
Or that the great theatre of Dionysius
could be aroused by some modern magic
                        to release
what is bound in it, stones!
that music might be wakened from them to
melt our ears   .

The sea is not our home   .

—though seeds float in with the scum
and wrack   .   among brown fronds
and limp starfish   .

Yet you will come to it, come to it!   The
song is in your ears, to Oceanus
where the day drowns   .

No! it is not our home.

You will come to it, the blood dark sea
of praise. You must come to it. Seed
of Venus, you will return   .   to
a girl standing upon a tilted shell, rose
pink   .

                         Listen!
Thalassa!   Thalassa!
            Drink of it, be drunk!
                    Thalassa
immaculata: our home, our nostalgic
mother in whom the dead, enwombed again
cry out to us to return   .
                    the blood dark sea!
nicked by the light alone, diamonded
by the light   .   from which the sun
alone lifts undamped his wings
                              of fire!

.   .   not our home!   It is NOT
our home.

                         What's that?
—a duck, a hell-diver?   A swimming dog?
What, a sea-dog?   There it is again.
A porpoise, of course, following
the mackerel   .   No.   Must be the up-
end of something sunk. But this is moving!
Maybe not. Flotsam of some sort.

A large, compact bitch gets up, black,
from where she has been lying
under the bank, yawns and stretches with
a half suppressed half whine, half cry .
She looks to sea, cocking her ears and,
restless, walks to the water's edge where
she sits down, half in the water   .

When he came out, lifting his knees
through the waves she went to him frisking
her rump awkwardly   .
Wiping his face with his hand he turned
to look back to the waves, then
knocking at his ears, walked up
to stretch out flat on his back in
the hot sand   .   there were some
girls, far down the beach, playing ball.

—must have slept.   Got up again, rubbed
the dry sand off and walking a
few steps got into a pair of faded
overalls, slid his shirt on overhand (the
sleeves were still rolled up) shoes,
hat where she had been watching them under
the bank and turned again
to the water's steady roar, as of a distant
waterfall   .   Climbing the
bank, after a few tries, he picked
some beach plums from a low bush and
sampled one of them, spitting the seed out,
then headed inland, followed by the dog

John Johnson, from Liverpool, England, was convicted after 20
minutes conference by the Jury. On April 30th, 1850, he was hung
in full view of thousands who had gathered on Garrett Mountain
and adjacent house tops to witness the spectacle.

This is the blast
the eternal close
the spiral
the final somersault
the end.

Book Five

To the Memory
of
HENRI TOULOUSE LAUTREC,
Painter

I

In old age
       the mind
            casts off
      rebelliously
     an eagle
from its crag

         — the angle of a forehead
             or far less
     makes him remember when he thought
         he had forgot

               — remember

         confidently
  only a moment, only for a fleeting moment —
       with a smile of recognition   . .

     It is early   . . .
    the song of the fox sparrow
 reawakening the world
   of Paterson
          — its rocks and streams
    frail tho it is
from their long winter sleep

     In March —
         the rocks
         the bare rocks
   speak!

— it is a cloudy morning.
     He looks out the window
        sees the birds still there —

Not prophecy! NOT prophecy!
                  but the thing itself!

                    — the first phase,
Lorca's *The Love of Don Perlimplín*,
            the young girl
                    no more than a child
leads her aged bridegroom
                innocently enough
                    to his downfall —

                    — at the end of the play, (she was a hot
little bitch but nothing unusual — today we marry women who are
past their prime, Juliet was 13 and Beatrice o when Dante first saw
her).

Love's whole gamut, the wedding night's promiscuity in the girl's
mind, her determination not to be left out of the party, as a moral
gesture, if ever there was one

    The moral

                proclaimed by the whorehouse
                    could not be better proclaimed
by the virgin, a price on her head,
                her maidenhead!
                    sharp practice
to hold on to that
                cheapening it:
                    Throw it away! (as she did)

    The Unicorn
                the white one-horned beast
                    thrashes about
root toot a toot!
                faceless among the stars
                    calling
for its own murder

Paterson, from the air
                    above the low range of its hills
                                across the river
on a rock-ridge
                    has returned to the old scenes
                                to witness

What has happened
                    since Soupault gave him the novel
                                the Dadaist novel
to translate —
                    The Last Nights of Paris.
                                "What has happened to Paris
since that time?
                    and to myself"?

A WORLD OF ART
THAT THROUGH THE YEARS HAS

SURVIVED!

— the museum became real
                    The Cloisters —
                                on its rock

casting its shadow —
                    "la réalité! la réalité!
                                la réa, la réa, la réalité!"

Dear Bill:

I wish you and F. could have come. It was a grand day and we
missed you two, one and all missed you. Forgetmenot, wild col-
umbine, white and purple violets, white narcissus, wild anemones
and yards and yards of delicate wild windflowers along the brook
showed up at their best. We didn't have hard cider or applejack
this time but wine and vodka and lots of victuals.   .   .   .   The

erstwhile chicken house has been a studio for years, one D.E. envied
when he saw it and it has been occupied by one person or another
writing every summer when I am here which has been pretty con-
tinuously for some time. The barn too has a big roomy floor which
anyone who finds a table and a chair in space enlivening is welcome
to. E.'s even fondled the idea of "doing something" about the barn
and I wish they would. Their kids went in bathing in the brook,
painted pictures and explored. If you ever feel like coming and get
transportation please come. E.'ll be up again before leaving Prince-
ton in June. They will be in H. next year. J.G. is occupying the
"Guest House" now.

How lovely to read your memories of the place; a place is made of
memories as well as the world around it. Most of the flowers were
put in many years ago and thrive each spring, the wild ones in some
new spot that is exciting to see. Hepatica and bloodroot are now
all over the place, and trees that were infants are now tall crea-
tures filled this season with orioles, some rare warbler like the
Myrtle and magnolia warblers and a wren has the best nest in the
garage (not to be confounded with any uptodate shelter) where I
had a coat lines with shipskin hanging and the wren simply used it
to back her nest against where she is sitting warm and pretty on
five eggs.

Best wishes and love from everyone who was here

                                                    Josie

            The whore and the virgin, an identity:
— through its disguises

    thrash about — but will not succeed in breaking free   :
                an identity
    Audubon (Au-du-bon), (the lost Dauphin)
                left the boat
                            downstream
    below the falls of the Ohio at Louisville
                to follow
    a trail through the woods
                across three states
                            northward of Kentucky . .

210

He saw buffalo
       and more
              a horned beast among the trees
in the moonlight
       following small birds
the chicadee
       in a field crowded with small flowers
.   .   its neck
       circled by a crown!
              from a regal tapestry of stars!
lying wounded on his belly
       legs folded under him
the bearded head held
       regally aloft   .
              What but indirection
will get to the end of the sphere?
       Here
is not there,
       and will never be.
              The Unicorn
has no match
       or mate   .   the artist
            has no peer .
Death
       has no peer:
wandering in the woods,
       a field crowded with small flowers
in which the wounded beast lies down to rest   .

       We shall not get to the bottom:
       death is a hole
       in which we are all buried
       Gentile and Jew.

The flower dies down
and rots away   .
But there is a hole
in the bottom of the bag.

It is the imagination
which cannot be fathomed.
It is through this hole
we escape   .   .

So through art alone, male and female, a field of
flowers, a tapestry, spring flowers unequaled
in loveliness.

Through this hole
at the bottom of the cavern
of death, the imagination
escapes intact.

.   he bears a collar round his neck
hid in the bristling hair.

Dear Dr. Williams:

Thanks for your introduction. The book is over in England be-
ing printed, and will be out in July sometime. Your foreword is
personal and compassionate and you got the point of what has
happened. You should see what strength & gaiety there is beyond
that though. The book will contain   .   .   .   I have never
been interested in writing except for the splendor of actual experi-
ence etc.   .   bullshit, I mean I've never been really crazy, con-
fused at times.

.   .   .   .

I am leaving for the North pole this time on a ship in a few weeks.
.   .   .   I'll see icebergs and write great white polar rhapsodies.
Love to you, back in October and will pass thru Paterson to see
family on way to a first trip to Europe. I have NOT absconded

from Paterson. I do have a whitmanic mania & nostalgia for cities and detail & panorama and isolation in jungle and pole, like the images you pick up. When I've seen enough I'll be back to splash in the Passaic again only with a body so naked and happy City Hall will have to call out the Riot Squad. When I come back I'll make big political speeches in the mayoralty campaigns like I did when I was 16 only this time I'll have W. C. Fields on my left and Jehovah on my right. Why not? Paterson is only a big sad poppa who needs compassion. . In any case Beauty is where I hang my hat. And reality. And America.

There is no struggle to speak to the city, out of the stones etc. Truth is not hard to find . . . I'm not being clear, so I'll shut up . . . I mean to say Paterson is not a task like Milton going down to hell, it's a flower to the mind too   etc   etc

A magazine will be put out . . . etc.

. . . .

Adios.

A.G.

IF YOU DON'T HAVE ANY TIME FOR ANYTHING ELSE
PLEASE READ THE ENCLOSED
SUNFLOWER SUTRA

> — the virgin and the whore, which
> most endures? the world
> of the imagination most endures:
>
> Pollock's blobs of paint squeezed out
> with design!
> pure from the tube. Nothing else
> is real   .   .
>
> WALK in the world
>   (you can't see anything
> from a car window, still less
> from a plane, or from the moon!? Come
> off of it.)

                    — a present, a "present"
world, across three states (Ben Shahn saw it
among its rails and wires,
and noted it down) walked across three states
for it   .   .
            a secret world,
a sphere, a snake with its tail in
its mouth
                    rolls backward into the past

. . .   The whores grasping for your genitals, faces almost
pleading . . .   "two dolla, two dolla" till you almost go in
with the sheer brute desire straining at your loins, the whisky and
the fizzes and the cognac in you till a friend grabs you . . .
"no . . .   to a real house, this is shit." A reel house, a real
house? *Casa real? Casa de putas?* and then the walk through the
dark streets, joy of livīng, in being drunk and walking with other
drunks, walking the streets of dust in a dusty year in a dusty cen-
tury where everything is dust but you are young and you are
drunk and there are women ready to love for some paper in your
pocket. Through the streets with dozens of bands of other soldiers
(they are soldiers even with civilian clothes, soldiers as you are
but different and this band is different because you are you — and
drunk and Baudelaire and Rimbaud and a soul with a book in it
and drunk) a woman steps into the open door of a café and puts
her hand between her legs and smiles at you . . .   at you a
whore smiles! And you yell back and all yell back and she yells
and laughs and laughter fills . . .   the . . .   guitar
soaked night air.

    And then the house, . . .   and see a smooth faced girl
against a door, all white . . .   snow, the virgin, ◯ bride
. . .   crook her finger and the vestal not-color of it, the
clean hair of her and the beauty of her body in the orchid stench,
in the vulgar assailing stench the fragility and you walk and sway
across the floor, and reel against the door and push away the voice
that embraces your ear dancers and find her, still standing against
the door and she is smooth-faced and wants four dollars but you

make it three but four she says and you argue and her hand on your
belly and she moves it and four and you can hear the music spin-
ning out its tropical redness the beer you gulp and touch the
breast, the firmness FOUR no three and smile a girl is carried out
of the room by a soldier (bride eternal) smile FOUR no three the
hand! the breast, you touch grasp hold lust feel the curve of a
buttock silent-smooth sliding under your palm, the dress, the hand!

High heels clack clack laughs nose and her eyes are black and
four? please and you pay four? no . three . and then yes
four, quatro . . . quatro dolares but twice, I go twice,
'andsome, come on, 'andsome. A child you follow her, the light
whirling in your eyes the noise the other girls in the babel friends'
voices unintelligible, edged with laughter the face at which you
smile though there is nothing to smile at but smile absurdly because
making love to a whore is funny but it is not funny as her blood
beneath flesh, her fingers fragile touch yours in rhythm not
funny but heat and passion bright and white, brighter-white than
lights of the whorehouses, than the gin fizz white, white and deep
as birth, deeper than death.

G. S.

    A lady with the tail of her dress
    on her arm . her hair is
    slicked back showing the round
    head, like her cousin's, the King,
    the royal consort's, young as she .
    in a velvet bonnet, puce,
    slanted above the eyes, his legs
    are in striped hose, green and brown.

    The lady's brow is serene
    to the sound of a huntsman's horn

— the birds and flowers, the castle showing through the leaves of
the trees, a pheasant drinks at the fountain, his shadow drinks there
also

                .   cyclamen, columbine, if the art
with which these flowers have been
put down is to be trusted — and
again oak leaves and twigs
that brush the deer's antlers   .   .
                the brutish eyes of the deer
                not to be confused
                with the eyes of the Queen
                are glazed with death   .
        .   a rabbit's rump escaping
through the thicket   .

One warm day in April, G.B. had the inspiration to go in swim-
ming naked with the boys, among whom, of course, was her
brother, a satyr if there ever was one, to beat anybody up who
presumed to molest her. It was at Sandy Bottom, near Willow
Point where in later years we used to have picnics. That was be-
fore she turned whore and got syphilis. L.M. about that time, a
young sailor, went to Rio unafraid of "children's diseases" as the
French (and others) called them — but it was no joke as Gauguin
found out when his brains began to rot away

        .   the times today
                are safer for the fornicators
                        the moral's
        as you choose but the brain
                need not putrefy
                        or petrify
        for fear of venereal disease
                unless you wish it

        "Loose your love to flow"
                while you are yet young
                        male and female
        (if it is worth it to you)
                'n cha cha cha
                        you'd think the brain
        'd be grafted
                on a better root

II

" . I am no authority on Sappho and do not read her poetry particularly well. She wrote for a clear gentle tinkling voice. She avoided all roughness. 'The silence that is in the starry sky,' gives something of her tone, . "

A. P.

Peer of the gods is that man, who
face to face, sits listening
to your sweet speech and lovely
    laughter.

It is this that rouses a tumult
in my breast. At mere sight of you
my voice falters, my tongue
    is broken.

Straightway, a delicate fire runs in
my limbs; my eyes
are blinded and my ears
    thunder.

Sweat pours out: a trembling hunts
me down. I grow paler
than dry grass and lack little
    of dying.

13 Nv/ Oke Hay my BilBill The Bul Bull, ameer

Is there anything in Ac Bul 2/ vide enc that seems cloudy to you, or INComprehensible/
    or that having comprehended you disagree with?

The hardest thing to discover is WHY someone else, apparently not an ape or a Roosevelt cannot understand something as simple as 2 plus 2 makes four.

217

McNair Wilson has just writ me, that Soddy got interested and started to study "economics" and found out what they offered him wasn't econ/ but banditry.

Wars are made to make debt, and the late one started by the ambulating dunghill FDR . . . has been amply successful.

and the stink that elevated him still emits a smell.

Also the ten vols/ treasury reports sent me to Rapallo show that in the years from departure of Wiggin till the mail stopped you suckers had paid ten billion for gold that cd/ have been bought for SIX billion.

Is this clear or do you want DEEtails?

That sovereignty inheres in the POWER to issue money, whether you have the right to do it or not.

don't let me crowd you.

If there is anything here that is OBskewer , say so.

don't worry re . . .

He didnt say you told him to send me his book, merely that he had metChu. let the young educ the young.

Only naive remark I found in Voltaire wuz when he found two good books on econ/ and wrote : "Now people will understand it." end quote.

But IF the buzzards on yr(and Del M's) list had been CLEAR I wdn't have spent so much time clarifying their indistinctnesses.

You agree that the offering da shittad aaabull instead of history is undesirable ??????

218

There is a woman in our town
walks rapidly, flat bellied
in worn slacks upon the street
where I saw her.
                        neither short
nor tall, nor old nor young
her
        face would attract no

adolescent. Grey eyes looked
straight before her.
                        Her
                                hair
was gathered simply behind the
ears under a shapeless hat.

Her
        hips were narrow, her
                                        legs
thin and straight. She stopped

me in my tracks — until I saw
her
        disappear in the crowd.

An inconspicuous decoration
made of sombre cloth, meant
I think to be a flower, was
pinned flat to her
                        right

breast — any woman might have
done the same to
say she was a woman and warn
us of her mood. Otherwise

she was dressed in male attire,
as much as to say to hell
with you. Her
                    expression was
serious, her
                    feet were small.

And she was gone!

.   if ever I see you again
as I have sought you
daily without success

I'll speak to you, alas
too late! ask,
What are you doing on the

streets of Paterson? a
thousand questions:
Are you married? Have you any

children? And, most important,
your NAME! which
of course she may not

give me — though
I cannot conceive it
in such a lonely and

intelligent woman

.   have you read anything that I have written?
It is all for you

                    or the birds   .
        or Mezz Mezzrow

                    who wrote   .

Knocking around with Rapp and the Rhythm Kings put the
finishing touches on me and straightened me out. To be with
those guys made me know that any white man if he thought
straight and studied hard, could sing and dance and play with the
Negro. You didn't have to take the finest and most original and
honest music in America and mess it up because you were a white
man; you could dig the colored man's real message and get in there
with him, like Rapp. I felt good all over after a session with the
Rhythm Kings, and I began to miss that tenor sax.

Man, I was gone with it — inspiration's mammy was with me. And
to top it all, I walked down Madison Street one day and what I
heard made me think my ears were lying. Bessie Smith was shout-
ing the *Downhearted Blues* from a record in a music shop. I flew
in and bought up every record they had by the mother of the blues
— *Cemetery Blues, Bleedin' Hearted,* and *Midnight Blues* — then
I ran home and listened to them for hours on the victrola. I was
put in a trance by Bessie's moanful stories and the patterns of true
harmony in the piano background, full of little runs that crawled
up and down my spine like mice. Every note that woman wailed
vibrated on the tight strings of my nervous system: every word
she sang answered a question I was asking. You couldn't drag me
away from that victrola, not even to eat.

                    .   .   or the Satyrs, a
        pre-tragic play,
                a satyric play!
                        All plays
        were satyric when they were most devout.
                Ribald as a Satyr!

        Satyrs dance!
                all the deformities take wing
                        Centaurs

leading to the rout of the vocables
in the writings
of Gertrude
Stein — but
you cannot be
an artist
by mere ineptitude
The dream
is in pursuit!
The neat figures of
Paul Klee
fill the canvas
but that
is not the work
of a child   .
the cure began, perhaps
with the abstraction
of Arabic art
Dürer
with his *Melancholy*
was aware of it —
the shattered masonry. Leonardo
saw it,
the obsession,
and ridiculed it
in *La Gioconda*.
Bosch's
congeries of tortured souls and devils
who prey on them
fish
swallowing
their own entrails
Freud
Picasso
Juan Gris.

a letter from a friend
    saying:
            For the last
three nights
    I have slept like a baby
        without
liquor or dope of any sort!
    we know
        that a stasis
from a chrysalis
    has stretched its wings   .
        like a bull
or a Minotaur
    or Beethoven
        in the scherzo
from the Fifth Symphony
    stomped
        his heavy feet
I saw love
    mounted naked on a horse
        on a swan
the tail of a fish
    the bloodthirsty conger eel
        and laughed
recalling the Jew
    in the pit
        among his fellows
when the indifferent chap
    with the machine gun
        was spraying the heap   .
he had not yet been hit
    but smiled
comforting his companions   .
    comforting
        his companions

223

                    Dreams possess me
                         and the dance
                                    of my thoughts
                 involving animals
                         the blameless beasts

(Q. Mr. Williams, can you tell me, simply, what poetry is?

A.   Well . . . I would say that poetry is language charged
     with emotion. It's words, rhythmically organized . . .
     A poem is a complete little universe. It exists separately. Any
     poem that has worth expresses the whole life of the poet. It
     gives a view of what the poet is.

Q.   All right, look at this part of a poem by E. E. Cummings, an-
     other great American poet:

                    (im)c-a-t(mo)
                    b,i;l:e

                    FallleA
                    ps!fl
                    OattumblI

                    sh?dr
                    IftwhirlF
                    (Ul)(lY)
                    &&&

     Is this poetry?

A.   I would reject it as a poem. It may be, to him, a poem. But
     I would reject it. I can't understand it. He's a serious man.
     So I struggle very hard with it — and I get no meaning
     at all.

Q.   You get no meaning? But here's part of a poem you your-
     self have written: . . . "2 partridges/ 2 mallard
     ducks/ a Dungeness crab/ 24 hours out/ of the Pacific/ and
     2 live-frozen/ trout/ from Denmark . . ." Now,
     that sounds just like a fashionable grocery list!

224

A. It is a fashionable grocery list.

Q. Well — is it poetry?

A. We poets have to talk in a language which is not English. It is the American idiom. Rhythmically it's organized as a sample of the American idiom. It has as much originality as jazz. If you say "2 partridges, 2 mallard ducks, a Dungeness crab" — if you treat that rhythmically, ignoring the practical sense, it forms a jagged pattern. It is, to my mind, poetry.

Q. But if you don't "ignore the practical sense" . . . you agree that it is a fashionable grocery list.

A. Yes. Anything is good material for poetry. Anything. I've said it time and time again.

Q. Aren't we supposed to understand it?

A. There is a difference of poetry and the sense. Sometimes modern poets ignore sense completely. That's what makes some of the difficulty . . . The audience is confused by the shape of the words.

Q. But shouldn't a word mean something when you see it?

A. In prose, an English word means what it says. In poetry, you're listening to two things . . . you're listening to the sense, the common sense of what it says. But it says more. That is the difficulty.

.   .   .   .   )

III

Peter Brueghel, the elder, painted
a Nativity, painted a Baby
new born!
among the words.

                Armed men,
savagely armed men
                armed with pikes,
halberds and swords
whispering men with averted faces
got to the heart
            of the matter
as they talked to the potbellied
greybeard (center)
the butt of their comments,
looking askance, showing their
amazement at the scene,
features like the more stupid
German soldiers of the late
war

— but the Baby (as from an
illustrated catalogue
in colors) lies naked on his Mother's
knees
— it is a scene, authentic
enough, to be witnessed frequently
among the poor (I salute
the man Brueghel who painted
what he saw —
          many times no doubt
among his own kids but not of course
in this setting)

The crowned and mitred heads
of the 3 men, one of them black,
who had come, obviously from afar
(highwaymen?)
by the rich robes
they had on — offered
to propitiate their gods

Their hands were loaded with gifts
— they had eyes for visions
in those days — and saw,
saw with their proper eyes,
these things
to the envy of the vulgar soldiery

He painted
the bustle of the scene,
the unkempt straggling
hair of the old man in the
middle, his sagging lips

— — incredulous
that there was so much fuss
about such a simple thing as a baby
born to an old man
out of a girl and a pretty girl
at that

But the gifts! (works of art,
where could they have picked
them up or more properly
have stolen them?)
— how else to honor
an old man, or a woman?

              — the soldiers' ragged clothes,
              mouths open,
              their knees and feet
              broken from 30 years of
              war, hard campaigns, their mouths
              watering for the feast which
              had been provided

              Peter Brueghel the artist saw it
              from the two sides: the
              imagination must be served —
              and he served
                            dispassionately

It is no mortal sin to be poor — anything but this featureless
tribe that has the money now — staring into the atom, com-
pletely blind — without grace or pity, as if they were so many
shellfish. The artist, Brueghel, saw them   .   :   the
suits of his peasants were of better stuff, hand woven, than we
can boast.

— have come in our time to the age of shoddy, the men are
shoddy, driven by their bosses, inside and outside the job to
be done, at a profit. To whom? But not true of the Portuguese
mason, his own boss "in the new country" who is building a
wall for me, moved by oldworld knowledge of what is "virtu-
ous"   .   "that stuff they sell you in the stores nowa-
days, no good, break in your hands   .   that manufac-
tured stuff, from the factory, break in your hands, no care
what they turn out   .   .   .")

    The Gospel according to St. Matthew, Chapter 1, verse 18, —
Now the birth of Jesus Christ was on this wise: When as his mother
Miriam * was espoused to Joseph, before they came together, she
was found with child of the Holy Ghost.

    * The King James version, of course, reads "Mary," but it is
recalled that Dr. Williams often referred to the mother of Jesus
as Miriam." Cf. the Hebrew Miryām as root for both names.—ED.
228

19   Then Joseph her husband, being a just man, and not willing to make her a publick example, was minded to put her away privily.

20   But while he thought on these things, behold, the angel of the Lord, appeared to him in a dream, saying, Joseph, thou son of David, fear not to take unto thee Miriam thy wife: for that which is conceived in her is of the Holy Ghost.

Luke   .   .   But Mary kept all these things, and pondered them in her heart.

                .   no woman is virtuous
            who does not give herself to her lover
            — forthwith

Dear Bill:

.   .   .   .

I am told by a dear friend in Paris, G.D. who is married to Henri Matisse's daughter, and who is the one vibrant head I have met in Europe, that France today is ruled by the gendarme and the concierge. In socialist Denmark I knew a highly intelligent author, a woman, who had come to America and there had a child by a wretched scribbler. Poor and forsaken she had returned to Copenhagen, where she earned her niggard indigence doing reviews for the Politiken, and giving occasional lectures on Middle English and early Danish. She lived in the slummy part of that beautiful city, trying to support a wonderful boy, sturdy, loving, and very masculine. It was my joy to bring him oranges, chocolate, and those precious morsels which his mother could not afford. She told me that the socialist police had called on her one night, asking why she had not paid her taxes to the government. Poverty was her reply. Do you recall the epitaph on Thomas Churchyard's tombstone?   .   .   .   'Poverty and Obscurity doth this tomb enclose.' A week later they returned, threatening to remove her furniture and have it impounded by the government. When she again pleaded that if she gave what Kroners she had her little boy would starve, the police said: 'We went to the Vin Handel last evening, and learned from the proprietor that you had bought a bottle of wine; if you can afford to drink wine you certainly can pay your taxes.' She then said 'I am so poor, and so driven to despair by it that I had to have a bottle of wine to relieve me of my melancholia.'

I am quite sure too that people only have the kind of government that their bellies crave. Furthermore, I cannot cure one soul in the earth. Plato took three journeys to Dionysius, the Tyrant of Syracuse, and once was almost killed and on another occasion was nearly sold into slavery because he imagined that he influenced a devil to model his tyranny upon The Republic. Seneca was the teacher of Nero, and Aristotle tutored Alexander of Macedon. What did they teach?

We are content here because it is cheap; my wife can eat chateaubriand for seven pesetas, about 15 or 16 cents. Going to the shops in the morning is a ritual; there is the greeting from the woman who runs the panadería, and the salutation (courtesy always eases the spirit and relieves the nervous system), from the man or his wife at the lechería (where you get milk, and an expansive smile from the humble woman who sells you three pesetas worth of helio, ice) . . . ,

Edward

Paterson has grown older

        the dog of his thoughts
has shrunk
to no more than "a passionate letter"
to a woman, a woman he had neglected
to put to bed in the past   .
             And went on
living and writing
        answering
letters
     and tending his flower
garden, cutting his grass and trying
to get the young
        to foreshorten

their errors in the use of words which
he had found so difficult, the errors
he had made in the use of the
poetic line:

"   .   the unicorn against a millefleurs background,   .   "

There's nothing sentimental about the technique of writing. It can't
be learned, you'll say, by a fool. But any young man with a mind
bursting to get out, to get down on a page even a clean sentence
— gets courage from an older man who stands ready to help him —
to talk to.

A flight of birds, all together,
seeking their nests in the season
a flock before dawn, small birds
"That slepen al the night with open yë,"
moved by desire, passionately, they
have come a long way, commonly.
Now they separate and go by pairs
each to his appointed mating. The
colors of their plumage are undecipherable
in the sun's glare against the sky
but the old man's mind is stirred
by the white, the yellow, the black
as if he could see them there.

Their presence in the air again
calms him. Though he is approaching
death he is possessed by many poems.
Flowers have always been his friends,
even in païntings and tapestries
which have lain through the past
in museums jealously guarded, treated
against moths. They draw him imperiously

to witness them, make him think
of bus schedules and how to avoid
the irreverent — to refresh himself
at the sight direct from the 12th
century what the old women or the young
or men or boys wielding their needles
to put in her green thread correctly
beside the purple, myrtle beside
holly and the brown threads beside:
together as the cartoon has plotted it
for them. All together, working together —
all the birds together. The birds
and leaves are designed to be woven
in his mind eating and   .   .
all together for his purposes

— the aging body
            with the deformed great-toe nail
makes itself known
            coming
                        to search me out — with a
                        rare smile
among the thronging flowers of that field
            where the Unicorn
                        is penned by a low
wooden fence
            in April!
                        the same month
when at the foot of the post
            he saw the man dig up
the red snake and kill it with a spade.
            Godwin told me
                        its tail
would not stop wriggling till
            after the sun
                        goes down —

232

he knew everything
              or nothing
                        and died insane
when he was still a young man

The (self) direction has been changed
              the serpent
                        its tail in its mouth
"the river has returned to its beginnings"
              and backward
                        (and forward)
it tortures itself within me
              until time has been washed finally under:
                        and "I knew all (or enough)
it became me   .   "
              — the times are not heroic
since then
              but they are cleaner
                        and freer of disease
the mind rotted within them   .
              we'll say
                        the serpent
has its tail in its mouth
              AGAIN!
                        the all-wise serpent

Now I come to the small flowers
              that cluster about the feet
                        of my beloved
      — the hunt of
              the Unicorn and
                        the god of love
      of virgin birth

The mind is the demon
drives us   .   well,
would you prefer it to
turn vegetable and

wear no beard?

— shall we speak of love
            seen only in a mirror
                        — no replica?
reflecting only her impalpable spirit?
            which is she whom I see
                        and not touch her flesh?

            The Unicorn roams the forest of all true
lovers' minds. They hunt it down. Bow wow! sing hey the
green holly!

— every married man carries in his head
            the beloved and sacred image
                        of a virgin
whom he has whored   .
                        but the living fiction
                                    a tapestry
silk and wool shot with silver threads
                        a milk-white one-horned beast
                                    I, Paterson, the King-self
saw the lady
                        through the rough woods
                                    outside the palace walls
among the stench of sweating horses
                        and gored hounds
                                    yelping with pain
the heavy breathing pack
                        to see the dead beast
                                    brought in at last

across the saddlebow
                among the oak trees.
                        Paterson,
keep your pecker up
                whatever the detail!
                        Anywhere is everywhere:
You can learn from poems
                that an empty head tapped on
                        sounds hollow
in any language! The figures
                are of heroic size.
                        The woods
are cold though it is summer
                the lady's gown is heavy
                        and reaches to the grass.

All about, small flowers fill the scene.
                A second beast is brought in
                        wounded.
And a third, survivor of the chase,
                lies down to rest a while,
                        his regal neck
fast in a jeweled collar.
                A hound lies on his back
                        eviscerated
by the beast's single horn.
                Take it or leave it,
                        if the hat fits —
put it on. Small flowers
                seem crowding to be in on the act:
                        the white sweet rocket,
on its branching stem, four petals
                one near the other to
                        fill in the detail

from frame to frame without perspective
                    touching each other on the canvas
                              make up the picture:
the cranky violet
          like a knight in chess,
                    the cinque-foil,
yellow faced —
          this is a French
                    or Flemish tapestry —
the sweetsmelling primrose
          growing close to the ground, that poets
          have made famous in England,
                    I cannot tell it all:
slippered flowers
          crimson and white,
                    balanced to hang
on slender bracts, cups evenly arranged upon a stem,
          foxglove, the eglantine
                    or wild rose,
pink as a lady's ear lobe when it shows
          beneath the hair,
                    campanella, blue and purple tufts
small as forget-me-not among the leaves.
                    Yellow centers, crimson petals
                    and the reverse,
dandelion, love-in-a-mist,
          cornflowers,
                    thistle and others
the names and perfumes I do not know.
          The woods are filled with holly
                    (I have told you, this
is a fiction, pay attention),
                    the yellow flag of the French fields is here
                    and a congeries of other flowers

as well: daffodils
        and gentian, the daisy, columbine
            petals
myrtle, dark and light
        and calendulas   .

The locust tree in the morning breeze
        outside her window
            where one branch moves
quietly
        undulating
            upward and about and
back and forth
        does not remind me more
            than of an old woman's smile
— a fragment of the tapestry
        preserved on an end wall
            presents a young woman
            with rounded brow
lost in the woods (or hiding)
        announced   .
            (that is, the presentation)
by the blowing of a hunter's horn where he stands
        all but completely hid
            in the leaves. She
interests me by her singularity,
        her courtly dress
            among the leaves, listening!

The expression of her face,
        where she stands removed from the others
— the virgin and the whore,
        an identity,
            both for sale

to the highest bidder!
           and who bids higher
                  than a lover? Come
out of it if you call yourself a woman.

I give you instead, a young man
           sharing the female world
                  in Hell's despight, graciously
— once on a time   .
           on a time:

           Caw!   Caw!   Caw!
                the crows cry!

           In February! in February they begin it.
           She did not want to live to be

           an old woman to wear a china doorknob
           in her vagina to hold her womb up — but

           she came to that, resourceful, what?
           He was the first to turn her up

           and never left her till he left her
           with child, as any soldier would

           until the camp broke up.

           She maybe was "tagged" as Osamu
           Dazai and his saintly sister

           would have it

She was old when she saw her grandson:
           You young people
                  think you know everything.

She spoke in her Cockney accent
                and paused
                            looking at me hard:
The past is for those that lived in the past. Cessa!

— learning with age to sleep my life away:
saying   .

        The measure intervenes, to measure is all we know,

                a choice among the measures   .   .

                            the measured dance
"unless the scent of a rose
                startle us anew"

Equally laughable
                is to assume to know nothing, a
                            chess game
massively, "materially," compounded!

                Yo ho! ta ho!

We know nothing and can know nothing   .
                            but
the dance, to dance to a measure
contrapuntally,
                Satyrically, the tragic foot.

Appendix

Book Six

These fragments of a projected sixth part of *Paterson* were found among Dr. Williams' papers after his death.

Jan. 4/ 61   Paterson 6

                    The intimate name you were known as
          to your intimates in that realm* was The Genius, before
your enemies got hold of you
          you knew the Falls and read Greek fluently
          It did not stop the bullet that killed you—close after dawn
          at Weehawken that September dawn

—you wanted to organize the country so that we should all
stick together and make a little money

                    a rich man

John Jay,   James Madison   .   let's read about it!

          Words are the burden of poems, poems are made of
                    words

     * realm? Original typescript reads "reaks."

the dandelion—lion's tooth-   in effigy
of faience, old Hudson River work, might as
well have been of Paterson

a crude cheap jar made to contain
pickled peaches or elder berries

casually with all the art of domestic
husbandry or the kitchen shelf
a royal blue curving
on itself to make a simple flower design

to decorate my bedroom wall

come out of itself to be an abstract design without design
to be anything but itself for a Chinese poet who
drowned embracing the reflection of the moon in the river

—or the image of a frosty elm outlined in gayest
of all pantomimes

Dance, dance! loosen your limbs from that art which holds you
faster than the drugs which hold you faster—dandelion on
my bedroom wall.

7/ 1/ 61

As Weehawken is to Hamilton
is to Provence we'll say, he hated it
of which he knew nothing and cared less
and used it in his schemes—so
founding the country which was to
increase to be the wonder of the world
in its day

which was to exceed his London on which he patterned it

(A key figure in the development)

       If any one is important more important that the
edge of a knife [= point of a dagger =] * a poem is: or an
irrelevance in the life of a people: see Dada or the murders of
a Stalin
       or a Li Po
                     or an obscure Montezuma

or a forgotten Socrates or Aristotle before the destruction of
the Library of Alexandria (as noted derisively by Bernard
Shaw) by fire in which the poems of Sappho were lost

    and brings us (Alex was born out of wedlock)

  illegitimately perversion righted through that alone
does not make a poet or a statesman

—Washington was a six foot four man with a weak voice and
a slow mind which made it inconvenient for him to move fast
—and so he stayed. He had a will bred in the slow woods so
that when he moved the world moved out of his way.

* Typed in above the line over "edge of a knife."

Lucy had a womb
                    like every other woman
                                    her father sold her
so she told me
                    to Charlie
                                    for 3 hundred dollars
she couldn't read or write
                    fresh out of
                                    the old country
she hadn't had her changes yet
                    I delivered her
                                    of 13 children
before she came around
                    she was vulgar
but fiercely loyal to me
                    she had a friend
                                    Mrs. Carmody
an Irish woman
                    who could tell a story
                                    when she'd a bit taken

New Directions Paperbooks—A Partial Listing

For complete listing request free catalog from
New Directons, 80 Eighth Avenue, New York 10011

† Bilingual

For complete listing request free catalog from
New Directons, 80 Eighth Avenue, New York 10011

† Bilingual